# Python Programming

AUTHOR

**Rupesh Nasre**
*Associate Professor*
Indian Institute of Technology (IIT)
Madras, Adyar, Chennai,
Tamil Nadu

REVIEWER

**Dr. Mahendran Botlagunta**
*Associate Professor*
VIT Bhopal University,
Madhya Pradesh

KHANNA BOOK
PUBLISHING CO. (P) Ltd.
4C/4344, Ansari Road, Darya Ganj,
New Delhi, India

All India Council for
Technical Education
Nelson Mandela Marg, Vasant Kunj,
New Delhi, India

Dear Readers,

To prevent the piracy, this book is secured with HIGH SECURITY HOLOGRAM on the front title cover. In case you don't find the hologram on the front cover title, please write us to at contact@khannabooks.com or whatsapp us at +91-99109 09320 and avail special gift voucher for yourself.

Specimen of Hologram on front Cover title:

Moreover, there is a SPECIAL DISCOUNT COUPON for you with EVERY HOLOGRAM.

How to avail this SPECIAL DISCOUNT:

Step 1: Scratch the hologram

Step 2: Under the scratch area, your "coupon code" is available

Step 3: Logon to www.khannabooks.com

Step 4: Use your "coupon code" in the shopping cart and get your copy at a special discount

Step 5: Enjoy your reading!

**ISBN:** 978-93-5538-745-5
**Book Code:** DIP441EN

**Python Programming**
*by* Dr. Rupesh Nasre

**First Edition:** 2025

*Originally Published by:*
**All India Council for Technical Education, Ministry of Education, GOI**

*Exclusively Published & Distributed by:*
**Khanna Book Publishing Co. (P) Ltd.**
4C/4344, Ansari Road, Daryaganj,
New Delhi (INDIA)

Visit us at: **www.khannabooks.com**
Write us at: **contact@khannabooks.com**

To view complete list of books,
Please scan the QR Code:

KPH

*Printed in Bharat.*

प्रो. म. जगदीश कुमार
अध्यक्ष
**Prof. M. Jagadesh Kumar**
**Chairman**

सत्यमेव जयते

आज़ादी का अमृत महोत्सव

अखिल भारतीय तकनीकी शिक्षा परिषद्
(भारत सरकार का एक सांविधिक निकाय)
(शिक्षा मंत्रालय, भारत सरकार)
नेल्सन मंडेला मार्ग, वसंत कुंज, नई दिल्ली–110070
दूरभाष : 011–26131498
ई–मेल : chairman@aicte-india.org

**ALL INDIA COUNCIL FOR TECHNICAL EDUCATION**
(A STATUTORY BODY OF THE GOVT. OF INDIA)
(Ministry of Education, Govt. of India)
Nelson Mandela Marg, Vasant Kunj, New Delhi-110070
Phone : 011-26131498
E-mail : chairman@aicte-india.org

## FOREWORD

Engineers are the backbone of the modern society. It is through them that engineering marvels have happened and improved quality of life across the world. They have driven humanity towards greater heights in a more evolved and unprecedented manner.

The All India Council for Technical Education (AICTE), led from the front and assisted students, faculty & institutions in every possible manner towards the strengthening of the technical education in the country. AICTE is always working towards promoting quality Technical Education to make India a modern developed nation with the integration of modern knowledge & traditional knowledge for the welfare of mankind.

An array of initiatives have been taken by AICTE in last decade which have been accelerate now by the National Education Policy (NEP) 2020. The implementation of NEP under the visionary leadership of Hon'ble Prime Minister of India envisages the provision for education in regional languages to all, thereby ensuring that every graduate becomes competent enough and is in a position to contribute towards the national growth and development through innovation & entrepreneurship.

One of the spheres where AICTE had been relentlessly working since 2021-22 is providing high quality books prepared and translated by eminent educators in various Indian languages to its engineering students at Under Graduate & Diploma level. For the second year students, AICTE has identified 87 books at Under Graduate and Diploma Level courses, for translation in 12 Indian languages - Hindi, Tamil, Gujarati, Odia, Bengali, Kannada, Urdu, Punjabi, Telugu, Marathi, Assamese & Malayalam. In addition to the English medium, the 1044 books in different Indian Languages are going to support to engineering students to learn in their mother tongue. Currently, there are 39 institutions in 11 states offering courses in Indian languages in 7 disciplines like Biomedical Engineering, Civil Engineering, Computer Science & Engineering, Electrical Engineering, Electronics & Communication Engineering, Information Technology Engineering & Mechanical Engineering, Architecture, and Interior Designing. This will become possible due to active involvement and support of universities/institutions in different states.

On behalf of AICTE, I express sincere gratitude to all distinguished authors, reviewers and translators from different IITs, NITs and other institutions for their admirable contribution in a very short span of time.

AICTE is confident that these out comes based books with their rich content will help technical students master the subjects with factor comprehension and greater ease.

(Prof. M. Jagadesh Kumar)

# ACKNOWLEDGEMENT

I am grateful to the authorities of AICTE, particularly Prof. M. Jagadesh Kumar, Chairman; Prof. M. P. Poonia, Vice-Chairman; Prof. Rajive Kumar, Member-Secretary and Dr Amit Kumar Srivastava, Director, Faculty Development Cell for their planning to publish this book on Python Programming. I am deeply indebted to Prof. Mahendran Botlagunta of VIT Bhopal University who promptly and thoroughly reviewed this book. His review significantly improved the presentation. The publication application in Unit 4 as well as Windows related commands are also due to his suggestions and guidance. I am thankful to Chinmay Nasre and AICTE Graphics Team for designing the cover page nicely.

I wrote this book from Nagpur, attending to my father's health, away from my wife and son. It was tough to meet the deadlines under the tight schedule amid hospital visits. But I am happy with the outcome. This book is dedicated to those *context-switches* between technical and non-technical matters.

This book is an outcome of various suggestions of AICTE members, experts and authors who shared their opinion and thought to further develop the engineering education in our country. Acknowledgements are due to the contributors and different workers in this field whose published books, review articles, papers, photographs, footnotes, references and other valuable information enriched us at the time of writing the book.

**Rupesh Nasre**

# PREFACE

This book is an introduction to Python Programming. Python is a popular programming language today and this book covers its basics. It is divided into five units, each of which builds upon the previous ones. The units span basics of variables and assignments all the way to developing web applications.

The first three units are required by all Python users. The units consist of the basic constructs and types, control constructs, and modular programming with functions and modules. Together, the three units equip a reader with the basic knowledge of Python to write simple programs. The fourth unit delves deeper into string functions, file handling, and regular expressions. Its programs are relatively little more complex and need more practice. I encourage readers to try out the programs in your own way prior to looking at the solutions. The fifth unit explores the Django framework to build web applications. Its configuration is also complicated. But I do hope you get the joy and satisfaction after you see your first web application running.

Each program explained in this book is available online on the book's webpage. The readers should (i) write the program themselves, (ii) then consult the readymade program, (iii) enhance the program with additional functionality.

Python has several libraries and frameworks, and more are developed regularly. The goal of this book is to make you hungry to learn more. I am sure you will have a good time learning through various carefully-crafted examples and illustrations. If you have any feedback to improve the book, feel free to write to me directly.

**Rupesh Nasre**

# OUTCOME BASED EDUCATION

For the implementation of an outcome based education the first requirement is to develop an outcome based curriculum and incorporate an outcome based assessment in the education system. By going through outcome based assessments, evaluators will be able to evaluate whether the students have achieved the outlined standard, specific and measurable outcomes. With the proper incorporation of outcome based education there will be a definite commitment to achieve a minimum standard for all learners without giving up at any level. At the end of the programme running with the aid of outcome based education, a student will be able to arrive at the following outcomes:

Programme Outcomes (POs) are statements that describe what students are expected to know and be able to do upon graduating from the program. These relate to the skills, knowledge, analytical ability attitude and behaviour that students acquire through the program. The POs essentially indicate what the students can do from subject-wise knowledge acquired by them during the program. As such, POs define the professional profile of an engineering diploma graduate.

National Board of Accreditation (NBA) has defined the following seven POs for an Engineering diploma graduate:

**PO1. Basic and Discipline specific knowledge:** Apply knowledge of basic mathematics, science and engineering fundamentals and engineering specialization to solve the engineering problems.

**PO2. Problem analysis:** Identify and analyses well-defined engineering problems using codified standard methods.

**PO3. Design/development of solutions:** Design solutions for well-defined technical problems and assist with the design of systems components or processes to meet specified needs.

**PO4. Engineering Tools, Experimentation and Testing:** Apply modern engineering tools and appropriate technique to conduct standard tests and measurements.

**PO5. Engineering practices for society, sustainability and environment:** Apply appropriate technology in context of society, sustainability, environment and ethical practices.

**PO6. Project Management:** Use engineering management principles individually, as a team member or a leader to manage projects and effectively communicate about well-defined engineering activities.

**PO7. Life-long learning:** Ability to analyse individual needs and engage in updating in the context of technological changes.

# COURSE OUTCOMES

By the end of the course the students are expected to learn:

**CO-1:** The necessary background in programming to solve problems using computation.

**CO-2:** Understand a given Python program and find what it does.

**CO-3:** Coding simple solutions to numeric and string problems.

**CO-4:** Using regular expressions to search for patterns in strings and files.

**CO-5:** Using Django to create simple web applications.

Mapping of Course Outcomes with Programme Outcomes to be done according to the matrix given below:

| Course Outcomes | Expected Mapping with Programme Outcomes (1- Weak Correlation; 2- Medium Correlation; 3- Strong Correlation) | | | | | | |
|---|---|---|---|---|---|---|---|
| | PO-1 | PO-2 | PO-3 | PO-4 | PO-5 | PO-6 | PO-7 |
| CO-1 | 3 | 3 | 3 | 3 | 1 | 1 | 3 |
| CO-2 | 3 | 2 | 2 | 2 | 1 | 1 | 3 |
| CO-3 | 3 | 2 | 2 | 2 | 1 | 1 | 3 |
| CO-4 | 3 | 2 | 2 | 3 | 1 | 1 | 3 |
| CO-5 | 3 | 3 | 3 | 3 | 1 | 1 | 3 |

## GUIDELINES FOR TEACHERS

To implement Outcome Based Education (OBE) knowledge level and skill set of the students should be enhanced. Teachers should take a major responsibility for the proper implementation of OBE. Some of the responsibilities (not limited to) for the teachers in OBE system may be as follows:

- Within reasonable constraint, they should manoeuvre time to the best advantage of all students.
- They should assess the students only upon certain defined criterion without considering any other potential ineligibility to discriminate them.
- They should try to grow the learning abilities of the students to a certain level before they leave the institute.
- They should try to ensure that all the students are equipped with the quality knowledge as well as competence after they finish their education.
- They should always encourage the students to develop their ultimate performance capabilities.
- They should facilitate and encourage team work to consolidate newer approach.
- They should follow Blooms taxonomy in every part of the assessment.

**Bloom's Taxonomy**

| Level | Teacher should Check | Student should be able to | Possible Mode of Assessment |
|---|---|---|---|
| Create | Students ability to create | Design or Create | Mini project |
| Evaluate | Students ability to justify | Argue or Defend | Assignment |
| Analyse | Students ability to distinguish | Differentiate or Distinguish | Project/Lab Methodology |
| Apply | Students ability to use information | Operate or Demonstrate | Technical Presentation/ Demonstration |
| Understand | Students ability to explain the ideas | Explain or Classify | Presentation/Seminar |
| Remember | Students ability to recall (or remember) | Define or Recall | Quiz |

## GUIDELINES FOR STUDENTS

Students should take equal responsibility for implementing the OBE. Some of the responsibilities (not limited to) for the students in OBE system are as follows:

- Students should be well aware of each UO before the start of a unit in each and every course.
- Students should be well aware of each CO before the start of the course.
- Students should be well aware of each PO before the start of the programme.
- Students should think critically and reasonably with proper reflection and action.
- Learning of the students should be connected and integrated with practical and real life consequences.
- Students should be well aware of their competency at every level of OBE.

# CONTENTS

# 1 Introduction, Variables and Data Types

## UNIT SPECIFICS

Through this unit we discuss the following aspects:

- History of the Python Programming Language
- Overall set of features supported by Python
- Basic setup and installation
- Basic data types, operators, input and output

## RATIONALE

This introductory unit gets readers acquainted with the basics of Python programming. It starts with a brief history of Python's creation. The unit then lists the language's overall set of features at a high level and motivates why it has become so popular. The unit then delves into basic language syntax, variables, and solves a few known problems in Python. We then introduce various data types such as numbers and strings and solve problems using those. We end this unit by introducing aggregate data types such as lists, tuples, and dictionaries. Care has been taken to introduce the readers to interesting problems despite the limitation of not having a conditional statement or a loop.

## PRE-REQUISITE

None

## UNIT OUTCOMES

List of outcomes of this unit is as follows:

**U1-O1:** Realize the history of Python

**U1-O2:** Implement simple program and execute it

**U1-O3:** Use different data types

**U1-O4:** Perform basic input and output

| Unit-1 Outcomes | EXPECTED MAPPING WITH COURSE OUTCOMES (1- Weak Correlation; 2- Medium correlation; 3- Strong Correlation) | | | | | |
|---|---|---|---|---|---|---|
| | CO-1 | CO-2 | CO-3 | CO-4 | CO-5 | CO-6 |
| U1-O1 | 3 | 3 | 3 | – | 3 | 1 |
| U1-O2 | 1 | 1 | 2 | 2 | 1 | – |
| U1-O3 | 2 | 1 | 3 | 1 | 2 | 1 |
| U1-O4 | – | – | 3 | 1 | 2 | 2 |

## 1.1 HISTORY

Python is a widely used programming language today. Starting from the first semester students to final year projects to industry personnel, Python finds its use in developing programs for graphics applications, text processing, data analysis, among others.

Python was developed by Guido van Rossam, a Dutch programmer, and released in 1991. The name is inspired from a BBC comedy show Monty Python's Flying Circus. Python is a successor of the ABC programming language. At the time of this writing, Python 3 is the latest major release of Python (on your computers, you may notice the program python3).

Since the last 20 years, Python has been in the Top 10 most popular programming languages. At the time of this writing (July 2022), Python is the most popular language, surpassing C and Java (according to the TIOBE index).

**Fig. 1.1:** "Two snakes" logo of Python

## 1.2 FEATURES

Python is a general-purpose programming language and supports multiple paradigms or ways of programming. For instance, we can write procedural (sequence of steps) as well as object-oriented programs (entities as objects and communication using messages across them) in it. It can also be used to write functional programs (applying and composing functions), among others. Unlike C and C++, Python is interpreted. This means Python programs are not compiled and stored into a binary code file (e.g., an executable)., but its source is translated into machine code and executed by the interpreter directly (without us seeing the executable code). Thus, on your computers, python3 is an interpreter (and gcc is a compiler for C programs).

Python is also dynamically-typed. This means that the type of a variable may not be specified in the source code, and is identified when the program executes. Python also relies on garbage collection which reclaims the allocated memory of the variables which are no longer needed (referenced, to be precise).

This relieves the programmer of the task of memory deallocation, similar to Java. Python also has a large variety of standard libraries, which allow us to write complex codes quickly, improving our productivity.

## 1.3 INSTALLATION AND EXECUTION

If you have access to the internet, you can write and execute Python programs online (e.g., Replit, CodeAcademy, Codevny). If you wish to install it on your laptop or iPad, you can download the appropriate installable for Windows or Linux or iPadOS or other operating systems from Python's official website www.python.org.

For instance, the following screenshot shows a Linux installation and running of Python.

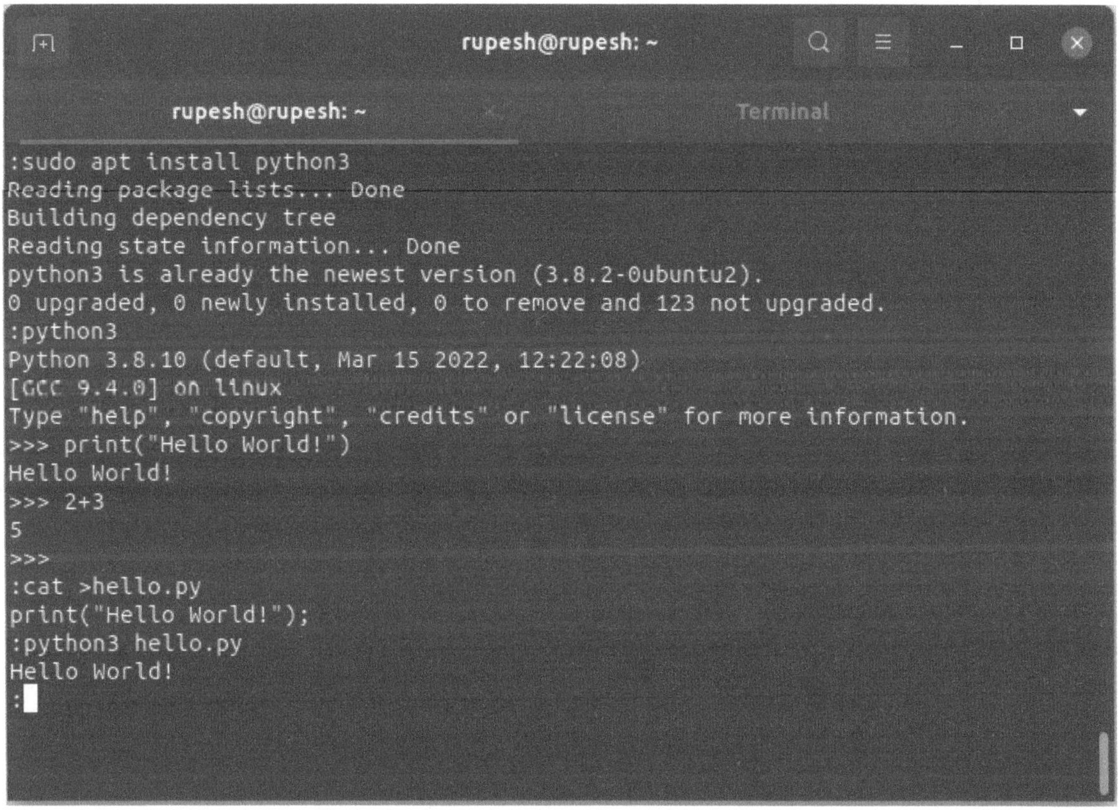


Once installed, you can invoke the Python interpreter (using graphical user interface or via a command line) to execute a Python program. Python programs can be written in your favorite editor (e.g., VS Code or Sublime or gedit or even notepad) apart from the Python IDE, called IDLE on Windows.

On the command line, you can use certain basic commands to navigate through the file system. For instance, if your home directory is /home/user, you can create a directory for Python programs as:

```
$ cd                                # go to home directory
$ mkdir python                      # create directory
$ cd python                         # go into that directory
$ cat >hello.py print("Hello World!") # create a new file hello.py
```

```
$ python3 hello.py          # run the Python interpreter
$ cd..                      # come back to home directory
```

Python programs are stored in files typically with extension .py (e.g., hello.py). On a command-line, we can execute the program as below.

```
$ python3 hello.py
```

In the above command-line, $ indicates the command-prompt, python3 is the interpreter, and hello.py is a text-file containing your program. On your computer, the interpreter name may differ depending upon your installation. For instance, on Windows, the interpreter binary is named python. Further, with new versions of Python, the binary name may change to python4.

## 1.4 HELLO WORLD!

A typical first program in a programming language prints Hello World! to the screen. Below is our first program in Python.

```
print("Hello World!")
```

The program uses a function print() to output a message to the screen. The message is given as an argument to print() and is specified in double-quotes ("). It can also be specified in single-quotes (') or triple-quotes (''' or """). When executed using the interpreter, it outputs the message.

```
$ python3 hello.py
Hello World!
$
```

The last $ indicates that the command-prompt is displayed again for the next command.

## 1.5 INPUT AND OUTPUT

The function print() is used for output, while the function input() is used for taking input from the user. Consider the following functionality where we wish to take the user's name as input and greet the user.

```
$ python3 greet.py
What is your name?
Guido van Rossam
Hello Guido van Rossam
$
```

One problem here is that we would like to greet exactly the name that was entered. This demands us to store the name during input and retrieve it during the output. Such an entity is called a variable. A variable is capable of storing a value which can be retrieved later. In fact, a variable can hold different values at different times. Our program achieving the above functionality looks like this.

```
1. print("What is your name?")
2. name = input()
3. print("Hello", name)
```

Note that the program is shown with line numbers, which are not part of the program. Line 1 prints our message asking for the user's name. Line 2 takes the input name and stores it in a variable called name. In Line 3, we use the same variable to greet the user.

You must have noticed that Lines 1 and 3 both use the print() function but take a different number of arguments (this is called polymorphism). In fact, the print() function can be invoked with an arbitrary number of arguments.

Another noteworthy point is that the printing on Line 3 automatically separates the two strings "Hello" and "Guido van Rossam" by a space (see the output above). This is the default behavior of print(). As another example, consider the following program.

```
print("Hello", "World!")
print("Bye", "World!")
```

What will be the output of the above program?

```
Hello World!
Bye World!
```

We specified neither the space nor the newline in our program. It is the default behavior of print(). This behavior can be changed with additional arguments to print().

```
1. print("Hello", "World!", end='####')
2. print("Bye", "World!", sep='$$')
3. print("With sep", "and end", sep=' ', end='.\n')
```

The output of the above program is

```
Hello World!####Bye$$World!
With sep and end.
```

Line 1 of the source code above prints the two strings separated by the default separator space ' ' but ends with '####'. Line 2 then prints the two strings separated by '$$' and ends with the default end-of-line character '\n'. Line 3 prints the two strings separated by space, which is explicitly specified, and ends with a full-stop followed by a newline. Thus, individual strings are separated by sep and the line is ended by end, whose default values are ' ' and '\n' respectively. '\n' is the newline character. Also note that strings are specified in this program with single as well as double quotes.

**Examples:**

| Program | Output |
|---|---|
| print('1', '+', '2', '=', '3') | 1 + 2 = 3 |
| print(1 + 2, 3/2) | 3 1.5 |

| Program | Output |
|---|---|
| print("a", "b", "c", "d", sep=",") | a, b, c, d |
| print("a" "b" "c" "d", sep=",") | abcd |
| id = "rupesh"<br>domain = "cse.iitm.ac.in"<br>print(id, domain, sep='@') | rupesh@cse.iitm.ac.in |
| id = "rupesh"<br>print(id, end='@')<br>print("cse", "iitm", "ac", "in", sep='.') | rupesh@cse.iitm.ac.in |

Consider a program wherein we wish to ask for a name and year of birth from a user, and then display the age of that user. We can write the initial part of such a program as follows.

```
print('Enter your name: ')
name = input()
print('Enter your year of birth: ')
yob = input()
```

When executed, the program works as follows.

```
Enter your name:
Guido van Rossam
Enter your year of birth:
1956
```

It will be nice if the input can be provided on the same line. This can be achieved as follows.

```
print('Enter your name: ', end='')
name = input()
print('Enter your year of birth: ', end='')
yob = input()
```

Another way to achieve it is by specifying the string as an argument to input().

```
name = input('Enter your name: ')
yob = input('Enter your year of birth: ')
```

When executed, the program works as expected.

```
Enter your name: Guido van Rossam
Enter your year of birth: 1956
```

Now let's get back to the task of calculating the age of the user. Thus, the program should be able to print the following (in the year 2023).

```
Enter your name: Guido van Rossam
Enter your year of birth: 1956
Hey Guido van Rossam you are 67 years old!
```

This can be achieved as follows.

```
name = input('Enter your name: ')
yob = input('Enter your year of birth: ')
print('Hey', name, "you are", (2023 - yob), "years old!")
```

Unfortunately, this simple program does not work. Why?

The Python interpreter considers variable yob to be of type string. Therefore, it cannot be directly used in arithmetic expressions (such as 2023 - yob). This means that the string "1956" is treated differently from the integer value 1956. To be used in an arithmetic expression, we need to convert the string "1956" into integer 1956. This can be done using the int() function.

```
name = input('Enter your name: ')
yob = input('Enter your year of birth: ')
print('Hey', name, "you are", (2023 - int(yob)), "years old!")
```

**Future connect:** Instead of hardcoding 2023 or the current year in the program, it would be nice if our program can find out the current year. This can be done using the datetime module, which we will study a little later.

Similar to string and int, there are other data types supported by Python. Let's take a look.

## 1.6 BASIC DATA TYPES AND OPERATORS

Python supports numeric types such as integer, floating point, as well as complex numbers. It also supports boolean values and strings. Further, the value of a variable can be converted from one type to another (as we saw in the last example).

**Example:** A card is drawn at random from a deck of well-shuffled cards. Find the probability of it being neither a king nor a spade.

We know that the deck has a total of 52 cards, split into 4 suites, each containing 13 cards. We can then compute the desired probability as follows.

```
ncards = int(52)
nkings = int(4)
nspades = int(13)
nspadeking = int(1)
nnonspadenonking = ncards - (nkings + nspades - nspadeking)
probnonspadenonking = nnonspadenonking / ncards
print('Probability of nonking, nonspade is', probnonspadenonking)
```

The output of this computation is:

```
Probability of nonking, nonspade is 0.6923076923076923
```

We can restrict the output to a few decimal digits using format specification (similar to C).

```
print('Probability is %f'  %probnonspadenonking,
                    '%.2f' %probnonspadenonking)
```

The output of these two lines alone (Lines 8 and 9) is:

```
Probability is 0.692308 0.69
```

Let's understand this formatted printing. Format specifier "%f" instructs printing of the next argument %probnonsadenonking to be a single-precision value which by default restricts the output to six decimal digits (unlike the original double-precision value). Format specifier "%.2f" restricts it further to 2 decimal digits. Note that there is no comma between the format specifier and %variable.

Another non-technical point this program reveals is about the variable names. As you may notice, the variables are difficult to read. One can use camelCase to improve it.

```
nCards = int(52)
nKings = int(4)
nSpades = int(13)
nSpadeKing = int(1)
nNonSpadeNonKing = nCards - (nKings + nSpades - nSpadeKing)
probNonSpadeNonKing = nNonSpadeNonKing / nCards
print('Probability of nonKing, nonSpade is', probNonSpadeNonKing)
```

**Good Programming Practice:** Use variable names that are easier to read and understand.

**Example:** Find the sum of the first n natural numbers.

We know the formula to compute the sum of the first n numbers: n * (n + 1)/2. Let us use this to write our program.

```
nstr = input()
n = int(nstr)
sum = n * (n + 1) / 2
print(sum)
```

We now understand that input() will return a string, which we need to convert to an integer (Line 2). After this, we apply the formula (Line 3) and print the sum. For input 10, the program should print 55.

```
10
55.0
```

From the output, it is clear that the computation is reasonable, but the sum is printed as a real number. This happens because the division operator (/) uses a floating point division. We can convert it to an integer in multiple ways.

```
n = int(input())
sum = n * (n + 1) / 2
print(int(sum))                 # using explicit conversion
print("%d" %sum)                # using format specifier
sum = n * (n + 1) // 2          # using integer division
print(sum)
```

Line 1 reads the input string, converts it into a number, and stores it in variable n. Line 2 computes the sum, which is by default a real value. We print it in Line 3 using the int() function. There is also a format specifier "%d" to print the value as an integer. We use that in Line 4. Alternatively, Python provides an integer division operator (//). On Line 5, we use it (now the same sum variable stores an integer value). We print the integer on Line 6.

The program highlights multiple points. First, types can be interconvertible. Second, a variable does not have a fixed type; it can have values of different types at different points in the program (e.g., variable sum). Hence, we do not declare them in Python. Third, notice comments on Lines 3 and 4 in gray font. Comments start with # and last till the end of that line. Comments are for improving the readability of the program and are not executed. Multiline comments in Python are often written using triple quotes.

**Good Programming Practice:** Use comments judiciously to improve the code readability.

**Examples:**

| Program | Output |
|---|---|
| print(5 + 3 / 4 - 2) | 3.75 |
| print(3.1 * 3.2 ** 3.3)<br># ** is an exponentiation operator<br># similar to Fortran | 143.99805374858647 |
| print("Last digit of 1234 is", 1234 % 10)<br># % is a modulus operator<br># which gives the remainder | Last digit of 1234 is 4 |

Python has inbuilt support for complex numbers. The following example conveys its syntax.

| Program | Output |
|---|---|
| x = 1 + 2j          # create | |
| y = complex(1, –2)          # create | |
| | |
| z = x – y          # arithmetic | |
| print(z) | 4j |
| | |
| z = x*y          # arithmetic | |
| print(z) | (5 + 0j) |
| print(z.real, '+', z.imag, 'j') | 5.0 + 0.0 j |

Lines 1 and 2 present two ways to create complex numbers (we can also read a complex number as a user input). Lines 4 and 7 illustrate simple arithmetic involving complex numbers. Finally, Line 9 shows how to separate its real and imaginary parts.

## 1.7 STRINGS

String is a fundamental data type in Python and the language provides many ways of manipulating strings. Strings are enclosed in single-, double-, or triple-quotes. Triple-quoted strings can span multiple lines. Certain characters such as '\n' have special meaning and are not treated as two characters, but one. These are called escape characters or escape sequences. Strings can be concatenated readily by using the + operator. Note that concatenation does not add a space between the two strings.

**Examples:**

| Program | Output |
|---|---|
| oneline = 'one line'<br>twoline = '''two lines''' # triple-quotes<br>print(oneline, twoline) | <br><br>one line two lines |
| errorline = "error line" # double-quotes | Syntax error |
| print("My drive is c:\nasre") # note \n<br>print("My drive is c:\\nasre") # escaped slash<br>print(r"My drive is c:\nasre") # raw string | My drive is c: asre<br>My drive is c:\nasre<br>My drive is c:\nasre |
| print("Tab\tseparated\ttext\non the second line") | Tab separated text on the second line |
| print('I don\'t understand quotes.')<br>print("I don't" 'understand' '''quotes.''')<br># quoted strings can be concatenated. | I don't understand quotes.<br>I don'tunderstandquotes. |
| oneline = 'one line'<br>print(oneline, oneline) # space-separated<br>print(oneline + oneline) # concatenated | <br>one line one line<br>one lineone line |
| print("My answer is", 3 * "No! ")<br>n = int(input())<br>print(n * "Python ") | My answer is No! No! No!<br>5<br>Python Python Python Python Python |

As the final example shows, strings can also be repeated easily with a multiplier.

Python provides a large set of operators and functions to manipulate strings. We illustrate this with a few examples below.

**Examples:** For the following set of examples, assume this initialization:

name = "Python Programming"

| ID | Program | Output |
|---|---|---|
| 1 | print(name[0], name[7], len(name)) | P P 18 |
| 2 | name[0] = 'C' | Syntax error |

| ID | Program | Output |
|---|---|---|
| 3 | print(name[-1], name[-11], name[-len(name)]) | g P P |
| 4 | first = name[1:5]<br>second = name[7:len(name)]<br>print(first, second, sep=',') | ytho,Programming |
| 5 | first = name[:6]<br>second = name[7:]<br>print(first, second, sep=',')<br>name = second + " " + first;<br>print(name) | Python,Programming<br><br><br>Programming Python |
| 6 | print(name[1::2]) | yhnPormig |

The first program with ID 1 indexes into the string name and extracts individual characters (which are actually one-length strings). Indexes start with 0. Thus, name[0] prints the first P. To find the length of a string, that is, the number of characters in it, len() function can be used. The last letter is at index len(name) – 1.

The program with ID 2 tries to modify the string by writing to name[0]. Incidentally, this is disallowed in Python (such strings are called immutable). If we want to modify a string, we need to assign the complete string. This is shown in the program with ID 5 where name is reassigned to a different string.

The program with ID 3 strangely uses negative indices! Python supports negative indexing whose meaning is counting backwards. Thus, name[–1] indexes the last character. Since this reverse indexing starts with –1, the first letter will be at index –len(name).

The program with ID 4 extracts substring. This can be done by specifying the index range [x:y] where all the characters starting with index x all the way upto-but-not-including y form the substring. Thus, name[1:5] includes name[1], name[2], name[3], and name[4] (ytho); it does not include name[5]. We can extract the second word with name[7:len(name)], which prints Programming. Note again that len(name) is an index one past the last letter's index.

The program with ID 5 extracts the two words from name. Not specifying the first index of the range defaults to 0, while not specifying the second index defaults to the length of the string.

The last program with ID 6 prints letters at odd indices. It starts from index 1 (letter y), goes up to the end of the string, and increments the index by 2.

**Example:** Extract fields from a roll number.

Consider an institute with roll numbers of the following format. An example roll number is CS23B010.

- The roll number is exactly eight letters long.
- The first two letters indicate the department (e.g., CS, ME, EE, AE).
- The next two digits indicate the admission year (e.g., 23, 22, 21, 20).
- The next letter is for degree (e.g., B for BTech, M for MTech, S for MS, P for PhD).
- The last three digits indicate the position within the class.

Our task is to extract these different fields from an input roll number. The solution program is given below.

```
rollno = input()                    # CS23B010
branch = rollno[0:2]                # CS
year = int(rollno[2:4])             # 23
degree = rollno[4]                  # B
position = int(rollno[5:8])         # 010
print(branch, "20%02d" %year, degree, position, sep='')
```

**Example:** Intelligent word shuffle

Find out what the below program does. The comments should help you decipher.

```
original = "eleven plus two"
first = original[:6]                # eleven
second = original[6:12] # plus
third = original[12:]               # two
first2 = first[:2]                  # el
first3 = first[2]                   # e
first45 = first[3:5]                # ve
first6 = first[-1]                  # n
third2 = third[:2]                  # tw
third3 = third[-1]                  # o
original = first2 + first3 + first45 + first6 + second + third2 + third3
modified = third2 + first2 + first45 + second + third3 + first6 + first3
print(original, "==", modified)
```

Python provides a variety of functions to manipulate strings (e.g., converting to upper-case, splitting based on a delimiter, substring search, etc.).

## 1.8 COMPOUND DATA TYPES

We now introduce the compound data types such as lists, tuples, and dictionaries. All these are aggregates of several elements (which could themselves be aggregates). We will make use of these later in an elaborate manner.

| Data type | List | Tuple | Dictionary |
|---|---|---|---|
| Properties | Ordered, allows duplicates, mutable | Ordered, allows duplicates, immutable | Associative, unique keys, mutable |
| Create | L = [0, 1, 2, "T", 4] | T = 0, 1, 2, "T", 4, 5 or T = (0, 1, 2, "T", 4, 5) | D={'IN':91,'US':1,'AU':7} or D = dict(IN=91, US=1, AU=7) or D = dict([('IN', 91), ('US', 1), ('AU', 7)]) |
| Index | L[0], L[-1] | T[0], T[-1] | D['IN'], D['AU'] |

| Data type | List | Tuple | Dictionary |
|---|---|---|---|
| Range/Slice | L[1:5] | T[1:5] | Not supported |
| Length | len(L) | len(T) | len(D) |
| Concatenation | L + L | T + T | D1 \| D2 (Python 3.9 onward) |
| Mutation | L[0] = 10 | Not supported | D['US'] = 2 |
| Append | L.append(6) | Not supported | Use mutation |
| Remove | L[2:12] = [] | Not supported | del(D['US']) |
| Unpack | e1, e2, e3 = L | e1, e2, e3 = T | e1, e2, e3 = D.items() |
| Others | Empty list as [] One length list as [1] | Empty tuple as () One length tuple as (1,) | Empty dictionary as {} One length dictionary as {0:'zero'} |

Note that in case of a list, L[2] = [] will not remove L[2]. Instead, it will replace L[2] with an empty list. Also note that one-length tuple is indicated with an extra comma, to distinguish it from a value, since (1) will be treated as parenthesized value 1.

A dictionary should be viewed as a storage for key-value pairs. The mapping from keys to values is captured in a dictionary.

**Future connect:** Following programs can be implemented in a generic way using loops.

**Example:** Store and print all the vowels from the word Mississippi.

Here, we will use a list to store the vowels.

```
word = "Mississippi"
vowels = []                    # empty list
vowels.append(word[1:2])
vowels.append(word[4:5])
vowels.append(word[7:8])
vowels.append(word[10:11])
print(vowels)
```

**Example:** Given a postal address, extract its fields, and print.

Here, we will make use of a string function called split() to divide a string into different parts, and make use of a tuple containing all the parts.

```
address = '670, New Nandanvan Layout, Near Sham Dham Temple, Nagpur, Maharashtra, 440024'
(plotNo, addrLine1, addrLine2, city, state, pincode) = address.split(', ')
print('Pincode =', pincode)
print('City = ', city)
```

**Example:** Extract the phone number of a friend from a directory.

We will implement a directory using a dictionary, with its key as the friend's name and its value as the friend's phone number.

```
phoneof = {'Rajesh':9432492125, 'Somesh':8793932633, 'JK':3283728272}
friend = input('Enter a friend\'s name: ')
print("The friend's phone number is", phoneof[friend])
```

## UNIT SUMMARY

We touched upon the historical aspects of Python's genesis and delved into writing simple programs using numbers and strings. We also introduced aggregates such as lists, tuples, and dictionaries.

## EXERCISES

### Multiple Choice Questions

**1.** What is the output of the following program?

```
print("p", "q", "r", sep='=')
```

(a) p = q = r  (b) p = q = r =
(c) = p = q = r  (d) = p = q = r =

**2.** Replace X in the following program such that the output is pqr#pqr.

```
print('pqr', X)
print('pqr')
```

(a) '#'  (b) """#"""
(c) sep='#'  (d) end='#'

**3.** What is the output of the following program if the input is 7.5?

```
cgpa = input("Enter your CGPA: ")
perc = 10 * cgpa
print(perc)
```

(a) 75  (b) Error
(c) 7.57.57.57.57.57.57.57.57.57.5  (d) 75.0

**4.** What is the output of the following program?

```
T = ("1", "1"+"1", "1"+"1"+"1", "1"+"1"+"1"+"1")
print(T[2])
```

(a) 1 1 1  (b) "3"
(c) 3  (d) 111

5. Replace X in the following program such that the output is 6.

```
M = {0:0, 1:1, 2:4, 3:9, 4:16}
M[X] = 9
M[5] = 25
print(len(M))
```

(a) 5 (b) 6
(c) 7 (d) 12

| ANSWERS | | | | | | | | | |
|---|---|---|---|---|---|---|---|---|---|
| 1. | (a) | 2. | (d) | 3. | (c) | 4. | (d) | 5. | (a) |

## PRACTICAL

1. Write a program that reads marks of three quizzes and outputs the total out of 100.
2. Read a string from the user. Assume these to be unique letters in a set. Find out the size of the powerset of this set. For instance, if the string is "abc", the set is {a, b, c} and its powerset is {{}, {a}, {b}, {c}, {a, b}, {a, c}, {b, c}, {a, b, c}} whose size is 8. For string "python", the output should be 64.
3. Write a program to find the probability of a card drawn from a standard deck to be neither a Spade nor a colored card (Jack, Queen, King).
4. Given a tuple of five coefficients e.g. (1, 2, –3, 0, 5), write the corresponding polynomial in x. For instance, $1x^4 + 2x^3 + -3x^2 + 0x + 5$.
5. Find the sum of the geometric series $1 + x + x^2 + x^3 + \ldots + xn$ given the values of x and n.

## Dynamic QR Code for Further Reading

# 2 Control Structures

## UNIT SPECIFICS

Through this unit we discuss the following aspects:

- Conditional processing using if, if-else, elif.
- Looping constructs for, while.
- Control-flow alteration using break, continue, pass, and else.

## RATIONALE

Assignment statements alone cannot enable us to write arbitrary programs. To write general-purpose codes, we need to alter the straight-line execution path, as well as execute certain statements repeatedly. This leads to conditional statements and looping constructs, which we study in this unit. Python also supports specialized variants, which allow us to systematically specify the desired control pattern.

## PRE-REQUISITE

Unit 1

## UNIT OUTCOMES

List of outcomes of this unit is as follows:

**U2-O1:** Use conditional constructs.

**U2-O2:** Use looping constructs.

**U2-O3:** Apply various control structures to solve problems.

| Unit-2 Outcomes | EXPECTED MAPPING WITH COURSE OUTCOMES (1- Weak Correlation; 2- Medium correlation; 3- Strong Correlation) | | | | | |
|---|---|---|---|---|---|---|
| | CO-1 | CO-2 | CO-3 | CO-4 | CO-5 | CO-6 |
| U1-O1 | 3 | 3 | 3 | – | 3 | 1 |
| U1-O2 | 1 | 1 | 2 | 2 | 1 | – |
| U1-O3 | 2 | 1 | 3 | 1 | 2 | 1 |

## 2.1 CONDITIONALS

Consider two millionaires: you and your friend. You want to identify who is richer. What do you do? While there are multiple ways to find this out, a direct way is to ask your friend the amount of property owned. You compare it with your property and find out the answer.

If we have to write this as steps of an algorithm (called pseudocode), we can do so using Python comments:

```
1. # ask your friend for the amount of property owned
2. # friend's property = read / listen from the friend
3. # my property = ....
4. # if my property > friend's property then
5. #     I am richer
6. # otherwise
7. #     Nevermind, I am not richer than my friend
```

Note how the outcome can differ depending upon the situation. Thus, the conditional check on Line 4 decides whether Line 5 is reached or Line 7. Also note that only one of the two is possible.

The above pseudocode is essentially computing the larger of two numbers, which could be two property evaluations, two digits, two ages, two times, or even two speeds. Irrespective of what we compare, the program pattern remains the same. Python allows us to write such a code using an if construct.

```
1. friendProperty = int(input('What is your property in millions? '))
2. myProperty = 10        # million
3. if myProperty > friendProperty:
4. print('I am richer.')
5. else:
6. print('Nevermind, I am not richer than you.')
```

Lines 3–6 present the syntax of an if-else statement. It evaluates the condition myProperty > friendProperty. Depending upon the value entered, this condition may evaluate to True or False. If the condition is True, Line 4 gets executed. If the condition is False, then Line 6 gets executed. Thus, the following two executions of the above program reveal the conditional execution of statements.

| What is your property in millions? 2<br>I am richer. | What is your property in millions? 15<br>Nevermind, I am not richer than you. |
|---|---|

Thus, the program when executed with input 2, evaluates the condition 10 > 2 to True, and hence, executes Line 4. In contract, with input 15, the program evaluates the condition 10 > 15 to False, and hence, executes Line 6.

Syntactically, the following points should be noted.

1. The condition of the if statement ends with a colon(:).
2. The else clause must end with another colon.

3. The else clause is optional. Thus, Lines 5 and 6 need not be present in the program and it is still a syntactically valid program.
4. There could be one or more lines in the if block and the else block. For instance, Line 4 forms the if-block, while Line 6 forms the else-block in the above program.
5. The if and the else blocks should be indented compared to the indentation of if-else.

**Example:** Matching blood group.

Let us say that the user enters two blood groups and we want to write a program to find out if the two blood groups match. While in reality, there are more matchings possible (e.g., $A^+$ can donate blood to $AB^+$), in our program, we will say that a blood group matches with only itself. Sample executions of such a program are as below.

| Enter the two blood groups: $A^+$ $A^+$<br>The two blood groups match. | Enter the two blood groups: $A^+$ $B^-$<br>It is a mismatch. |
|---|---|

```
1. bg1, bg2 = input("Enter the two blood groups:").split()
2. if bg1 == bg2:
3. print("The two blood groups match.")
4. else:
5. print("It is a mismatch.")
```

We use the split() function to read two blood groups separated by spaces, and assign those to two variables in the same assignment statement (Line 1). We then check if the two blood groups entered are the same. This is done using the == operator, for checking equality. If the two blood groups are the same, the condition evaluates to True, leading to execution of Line 3. Otherwise, Line 5 gets executed.

The following table shows various comparison operators available in Python.

| Op | Meaning | Usage |
|---|---|---|
| < | Less than | if a < b: print('a is smaller') |
| > | Greater than | if a > b: print('a is larger') |
| <= | Less than or equal to | if a <= b: print('a is less than or equal to b') |
| >= | Greater than or equal to | if a >= b: print('a is greater than or equal to b') |
| == | Equal to | if a == b: print('a and b are equal') |

The above table also illustrates that the else clause is optional.

**Example:** Find the student from your department.

Say you are in the Computer Science (CS) Department with roll number as CS23B001. Using the roll number of a student, you should be able to find out if the student is from CS or not. It should work as follows.

| Your roll number: CS23B010<br>Hi Bro! | Your roll number: ME23B111<br>Excuse me? |
|---|---|

| Your roll number: CH23B002 | Your roll number: BS23B002 |
|---|---|
| Excuse me? | Excuse me? |

Let's write a program for it. The input is a string holding the roll number. We need to extract the first two characters (how?) and check if those are 'C' and 'S'. This can be done using nested if-else statements.

```
1. rollNum = input("Your roll number: ")
2. if rollNum[0] == 'C':
3. if rollNum[1] == 'S':
4. print("Hi Bro!")
5. else:
6. print("Excuse me?")
```

Note the extra indentation for Line 4, due to the nesting. If the first character is 'C', it checks the second character on Line 3, and if it is 'S', then it executes Line 4. Otherwise, it executes Line 6. Out of the four inputs given above, try running this program with those inputs. For which inputs the program gives the expected output?

You would notice that this program gives the correct output for CS23B010, ME23B111, BS23B002, but does not produce any output for CH23B002. Why? Well, because we did not ask it to. The else clause on Line 5 corresponds to the if clause on Line 2. As far as the if clause of Line 3 is concerned, it does not have an associated else clause. Hence, when the condition on Line 3 is False (CH....), the control comes out of the nested-if statement without any output. How do we fix it?

```
1. rollNum = input("Your roll number: ")
2. if rollNum[0] == 'C':
3. if rollNum[1] == 'S':
4. print("Hi Bro!")
5. else:
6. print("Excuse me?")
```

The code is still wrong. For what input does it produce no output?

Out of the four inputs, the program produces correct output for CS23B010 and CH23B002. But it does not produce any output for ME... and BS... roll numbers. This is because, due to indentation, the else clause now corresponds to the if clause on Line 3. Line 2 does not have any corresponding else. So let's add it.

```
1. rollNum = input("Your roll number: ")
2. if rollNum[0] == 'C':
3.     if rollNum[1] == 'S':
4.         print("Hi Bro!")
5.     else:
6.         print("Excuse me?")
7. else:
8.     print("Excuse me?")
```

Now the program works across all the inputs. But note that there is a duplicate processing on Lines 6 and 8. Can we avoid this duplication?

## Conjuncts

The duplication can be avoided if we can combine the if conditions on Lines 2 and 3. Python allows us to do that using conjuncts such as and and or.

```
1. rollNum = input("Your roll number: ")
2. if rollNum[0] == 'C' and rollNum[1] == 'S':
3.     print("Hi Bro!")
4. else:
5.     print("Excuse me?")
```

The conjunct executes the if-block if both the conditions are true. Otherwise, it executes the else-block. Line 2 can also be written succinctly as:

2. if rollNum[0:2] == 'CS':

**Example:** Find the student from your department where the roll number may be in capital or small-case letters.

To address this, we need to augment our if condition to include small-case letters too.

```
1. rollNum = input("Your roll number: ")
2. if (rollNum[0] == 'C' or rollNum[0] == 'c') and (rollNum[1] == 'S' or rollNum[1] == 's'):
3.     print("Hi Bro!")
4. else:
5.     print("Excuse me?")
```

Thus, the or conjunct evaluates to True if any one of the conditions evaluates to True. That is, it evaluates to False only if all the conditions are False.

Note the use of parentheses to combine the clauses by the and conjunct. This is required because or has a lower precedence than the and conjunct. Thus, in absence of parentheses, the meaning of Line 2 would be:

2. if rollNum[0] == 'C' or (rollNum[0] == 'c' and rollNum[1] == 'S') or rollNum[1] == 's':

Can you find out the inputs for which this modified program would produce wrong results?

One may write the above program by reordering the conditions.

```
1. rollNum = input("Your roll number: ")
2. if (rollNum[0] == 'C' and rollNum[1] == 'S') or \
3.    (rollNum[0] == 'c' and rollNum[1] == 's'):
4.     print("Hi Bro!")
5. else:
6.     print("Excuse me?")
```

Are the last two programs equivalent? The answer is no. The last program allows roll numbers 'CS...' and 'cs...', but does not allow a mixed-case 'Cs...' or 'cS...', which is permitted by the earlier program.

Also note how the long statement on Line 2 is split using a backslash at the end of the line. Without the backslash, the program exhibits a syntax error.

Yet another way in which the above check can be made is by using a string function upper(), which returns its upper-case version. The following program illustrates this.

```
rollNum = input("Your roll number: ")
if rollNum[0:2].upper() == 'CS':
   print("Hi Bro!")
else:
   print("Excuse me?")
```

Is it possible to print "Excuse me?" in the if-block and "Hi Bro!" in the else-block? This demands reversing the conditions. Python provides the not keyword to alter the truth-value of a condition. Thus, the functionally equivalent program would be:

```
rollNum = input("Your roll number: ")
if not (rollNum[0:2].upper() == 'CS'):
   print("Excuse me?")              # note the exchange of print() statements
else:
   print("Hi Bro!")
```

When the program execution finds out that rollNum[0] is not 'C', does it need to check if rollNum[1] is 'S' or not? It does not need to, since the truth value of the condition is anyway going to be False. This way of evaluating conditions is called short-circuiting.

## Short-circuiting

In short-circuiting, only as many sub-conditions as required to find the truth value of the whole condition are evaluated. This can lead to some sub-conditions not getting evaluated. We explain this using an example: a == 0 and (b < 3 or c <= 5). In the below table, ✓ indicates that the corresponding sub-condition is evaluated. An empty cell indicates that the sub-condition is short-circuited and, therefore, not evaluated.

| Values | a == 0 | b < 3 | c <= 5 | Truth value |
|---|---|---|---|---|
| a = 0, b = 3, c = 6 | √ | √ | √ | False |
| a = 0, b = 3, c = 5 | √ | √ | √ | True |
| a = 0, b = 2, c = 5 | √ | √ | | True |
| a = 0, b = 2, c = 6 | √ | √ | | True |
| a = 1, b = 3, c = 5 | √ | | | False |

Thus, when a = 0, b = 2, c = 6, the sub-condition a == 0 is evaluated and is True. However, we cannot deduce whether the whole condition is True or not, due to the presence of the and conjunct.

Therefore, we must evaluate (b < 3 or c <= 5). The sub-condition, b < 3 is True. At this stage, we can say that therefore, the condition (b < 3 or c <= 5) is also True – without evaluating c <= 5. Thus, the last sub-condition gets short-circuited and is not evaluated. The whole condition evaluates to True.

Note that a row such as the following is not possible for this example.

| a = ..., b = ..., c = ... | ✓ | ✓ | | False |
|---|---|---|---|---|

One may wonder how such a phenomenon affects you, since this seems to be only an optimization and not affecting any output. The output gets affected when sub-conditions can have side-effects. For instance, if a, b, c are replaced with function calls, and each function has a print() statement, then the output will depend upon whether the short-circuiting happens or not.

**Future connect:** We will study functions in detail in another unit. But to illustrate short-circuiting, we present an example using functions.

```
1.  def a():
2.  print(“a”)
3.  return True
4.  def b():
5.  print(“b”)
6.  return True
7.  def c():
8.  print(“c”)
9.  return True
10.
11. if a() and (b() or c()):
12. print(“Whole condition is true.”)
13. else:
14. print(“Whole condition is false.”)
```

The above program defines three functions a(), b() and c(), which print a message and return True. The main program starts from Line 11 (similar to our programs so far), and evaluates the condition. After evaluating function a() and function b(), the condition is guaranteed to be True, hence, function c() is not executed. Therefore, the output of the above code is:

```
a
b
Whole condition is true.
```

Without short-circuiting, c would also have been printed.

Does this mean short-circuiting is useful only while using functions? Not at all. Short-circuiting can be very useful to guard against an invalid access. For instance, consider the condition below:

```
if index < len(mystring) and mystring[index] == ‘x’:
```

With short-circuiting, if the index is beyond the string then the first sub-condition is False. Therefore, the second sub-condition will not be evaluated, avoiding the out-of-bound access.

**Example:** Lucky cards!

To expand on our understanding, let's implement the game of lucky cards. We know that a standard deck of 52 cards is grouped into four suites Club, Diamond, Heart, and Spade, each containing 13 cards: Ace, 2, 3, 4, 5, 6, 7, 8, 9, 10, Jack, Queen, and King. Some of these cards are considered lucky. Our task is to read a card as input and output if the card is lucky or not.

The predefined set of lucky cards is as follows:

- Ace of Spade
- Any Heart
- Queen of Diamond
- King of Diamond
- Any 7

The corresponding program will have a list of conditions separated by or. Each condition can then take care of one category of lucky cards. A sample run of such a program can be as follows.

```
Enter your card: 7 of Heart
Lucky you!
Enter your card: Queen of Spade
Better luck next time.
Enter your card: 8 of Spade
Better luck next time.
Enter your card: Ace of Spade
Lucky you!
```

Let's write the program using conditionals for lucky cards.

```
1.  card, of, suite = input('Enter your card: ').split()
2.
3.  if (suite == 'Spade' and card == 'Ace')          or \
4.  (suite == 'Heart')                               or \
5.  (suite == 'Diamond' and card == 'Queen')         or \
6.  (suite == 'Diamond' and card == 'King')          or \
7.  (card == '7'):
8.  print('Lucky you!')
9.  else:
    print('Better luck next time.')
```

Line 1 uses the split() method to separate the three words, and accordingly, find the suite and the card in it. It then runs a large if condition, separated by or, split on multiple lines connected by backslash (\). If any one of the conditions is satisfied, it is a lucky card. Note that Line 7 should use string '7' and not integer 7.

We would like to now enhance this program to check for invalid cards. Thus, inputs such as 'seven of Spade' or '7 of spade' or '7 Spade' or '11 of Spade' should be marked as invalid.

```
1.  card, of, suite = input('Enter your card: ').split()
2.
3.  if (suite != 'Spade' and suite != 'Heart' and \
4.      suite != 'Club' and suite != 'Diamond') or \
5.     (card != 'Ace' and card != '2' and card != '3' and card != '4' and \
6.      card != '5' and card != '6' and card != '7' and card != '8' and \
7.      card != '10' and card != 'Jack' and card != 'Queen' and card != 'King'):
8.      print('Invalid card')
9.
10. elif (suite == 'Spade' and card == 'Ace')          or \
11.       (suite == 'Heart')                           or \
12.       (suite == 'Diamond' and card == 'Queen')     or \
13.       (suite == 'Diamond' and card == 'King')      or \
14.       (card == '7'):
15.       print('Lucky you!')
16. else:
17.       print('Better luck next time.')
```

In the above program, Line 1 and Lines 10 – 17 remain the same as before, except replacing if on Line 10 with elif. In addition we create another long condition to check if the card is invalid. This is done with subconditions to check the suite (Lines 3 and 4) and subconditions to check the card (Lines 5 – 7). The two subconditions are joined with an or condition (end of Line 4, and note the parentheses).

The condition can be simplified using De Morgan's laws. The laws mention:

not x and not y == not(x or y)

not x or not y == not(x and y)

Thus, Lines 3–8 can be rewritten as:

```
3. if not ( (suite == 'Spade' or suite == 'Heart' or \
4. suite == 'Club' or suite == 'Diamond') and \
5. (card == 'Ace' or card == '2' or card == '3' or card == '4' or \
6. card == '5' or card == '6' or card == '7' or card == '8' or \
7. card == '10' or card == 'Jack' or card == 'Queen' or card == 'King') ):
8. print('Invalid card')
```

Carefully note the application of the laws. The inner subconditions now contain ==, which are easier to decipher. The conditions of the suite and the card are joined using an and while the subconditions of a suite are joined using or. If the big condition is true, it means that it is a valid card. Therefore, to check invalidity, a negation using not is required for the whole condition (note the parentheses).

## 2.2 Loops

Some programs cannot be written without the ability to repeat. For instance, consider printing 'Hello World!' 100 times. One can write 100 print() statements easily. However, if I now ask you to write a program to take a number from the user and print 'Hello World!' those many times, you would be stuck!

Loops allow us to repeat an arbitrary piece of code, arbitrarily number of times. Python supports two types of loops: while and for. The while loop iterates through (repeats) a sequence of code till a given condition is True. The for loop iterates over the items of a given sequence. We will study both in detail now.

## While Loop

Let's first write our program to print a message a certain user-defined number of times.

```
1. n = int(input())
2. i = 0
3. while i < n:
4. print('Hello World!')
```

Note the similarity of the loop's structure with that of an if statement. The body of the loop (in this case, Line 4) is repeated till the condition on Line 3 is true.

If you enter 10 as input, how many 'Hello World!'s does our program print? 9 or 10?

Well, it continues to print 'Hello World!' an unbounded number of times. Why? Because we asked it to. The condition i < n continues to remain true, as the value of i never changes in the loop. To get the expected result, we need to increment i.

```
n = int(input())
i = 0
while i < n:
print('Hello World!')
i = i + 1                    # progress
```

**Remember:**A loop must make progress towards its terminating condition.

**Example:** Find pass-percentage of a class.

A teacher is entering the marks of students. A student passes a course if the marks are at least 40 (out of 100). The teacher wants to know the percentage of students passed.

```
n = int(input('Number of students: '))
i = 0
pass = 0

while i < n:                          # predefined number of iterations
marks = int(input('Enter marks: '))

if marks >= 40:
pass = pass + 1

i = i + 1

print(pass * 100 / n, '% passed')
```

To find the pass percentage, we need the number of students P passing the course, and the total number of students N in the class. The output then is P*100/N. Finding P needs us to go through all the marks. How do you find N?

There are two ways. One, we ask the teacher to enter N at the start of our program. Two, we derive it based on a special end-of-class marker (e.g., –1 for marks). Let's write the program both ways.

Note how we added blank lines 4, 7, and 10, which makes the code tidy and often easier to understand. The code can be enhanced to check for the divide-by-zero error at Line 13.

**Good Programming Practice:** Add blank lines to improve readability of the code. A typical convention is to have a blank line prior to and after a control construct (and functions), especially for large programs.

Let's now write it with an end-of-class marker. Assuming marks are always non-negative (no negative marking by the teacher), we can use –1 as a special marker. As soon as that number is entered, our program can know that marks of all the students are entered and we can now compute the percentage.

A sample execution of such a program would be as follows.

```
Enter marks: 5
Enter marks: 10
Enter marks: 50
Enter marks: 32
Enter marks: 23
Enter marks: 40
Enter marks: 89
Enter marks: 100
Enter marks: 99
Enter marks: 89
Enter marks: -1
60.0 % passed
```

The output was computed by counting the number of non-negative inputs as N. The corresponding program is as follows.

```
1.  n = 0
2.  pass = 0
3.  marks = int(input('Enter marks: '))
4.
5.  while marks >= 0:            # number of iterations based on data
6.  if marks >= 40:
7.  pass = pass + 1
8.
9.  n = n + 1
10. marks = int(input('Enter marks: '))
11.
12. print(pass * 100 / n, '% passed')
```

Note how the condition changed at Line 5. It is now based on the marks entered. The students are counted at Line 9. Note also the usage of the same statement at Lines 3 and 10. You will find this to be a recurrent pattern.

One can use tricks to avoid the repetition. For instance, by initializing n to -1, marks to 0, and removing the input() statement outside the loop. The code will be functionally equivalent to the above code. But it is important to make sure that the code is readable.

**Example:** Print Fibonacci sequence.

Fibonacci sequence is defined as follows.

Fib(0) = 0, Fib(1) = 1

Fib(n) = Fib(n – 1) + Fib(n – 2)

If we expand the Fib function, we get a sequence as 0, 1, 1, 2, 3, 5, 8, 13, 21, 34, … Since it is unending, we can specify how many terms you wish to print, that is, the value of n.

**Future Connect:** Fibonacci sequence is a classic example of recursion.

While Fibonacci numbers have a strong presence in Mathematics, a few natural phenomena also follow Fibonacci numbers (e.g., how branches emerge in trees or how petals of certain flowers are arranged).

Can we use loops to print this sequence? We can get started like this (as a pseudocode).

```
n = int(input())
first number = 0
second number = 1
while n > 0:
print the first number
Shall I print the second number?
sum = first number + second number
What happens in the second iteration?
n = n - 1
```

The issues need to be resolved as follows.

- We should print only one number per iteration.
- Somehow, the first number should take the next value to be printed in the next iteration.
- The other two variables (second number and sum) should be computed but not printed in the current iteration.

Essentially, the Fibonacci sequence should slide through the three variables.

| first number | second number | sum |
|---|---|---|
| 0 | 1 | 1 |
| 1 | 1 | 2 |
| 1 | 2 | 3 |
| 2 | 3 | 5 |
| 3 | 5 | 8 |
| 5 | 8 | 13 |
| … | … | … |

This sliding through can be implemented by:

- discarding the printed value of the first number,
- storing second number into the first number, and
- storing sum into the second number.

The overall program now becomes:

```
1. n = int(input())
2. first = 0
3. second = 1
4.
5. while n > 0:
6. print(first)
7. sum12 = first + second
8. first = second
9. second = sum12
10. n = n - 1
```

Note the order of statements 7, 8, and 9. Reordering of these statements would result in a wrong output. By the way, we can use sum instead of sum12 and the code would work. But since sum() is a predefined function in Python, we would like to avoid using the same name.

The same code can be succinctly written using the multiple-assignment form, which gets rid of the sum12 variable.

```
n = int(input())
first, second = 0, 1

while n > 0:
print(first)
first, second = second, first + second
n = n - 1
```

It is important to understand that for the program to work correctly, all the expressions on the right hand side of = must be evaluated before any assignment to the left hand side variables happens. This allows you to swap two variables easily: x, y = y, x

**Example:** Collatz sequence.

Mathematician Collatz made a conjecture which is still unproven. He said, start from any positive integer. If it is even, halve it; otherwise triple it and add one. Now repeat this process. This sequence will finally reach 1. This conjecture is also known as the 3n + 1 problem. For instance, for input 7, the sequence becomes 7, 22, 11, 34, 17, 52, 26, 13, 40, 20, 10, 5, 16, 8, 4, 2, 1.

Let's implement this sequence given an input number.

```
n = int(input())

while n != 1:
if n % 2 == 1:
n = 3 * n + 1
else:
n = n // 2
print(n)

print('How do I always get printed?')
```

## For Loops

For loops work with an ordered sequence, wherein the loop variable assumes the value of each element in the sequence from left to right in different iterations. For instance, the simple form of a for loop can be used to print numbers from 0 to 9.

```
for i in range(10):
print(i)
```

In the above program, i is the loop variable, going over the sequence returned by range(). The function could also be used to step through the sequence in a strided manner. For instance, consider the following code.

```
for i in range(10, 20, 3):
print(i)
```

Its output is

```
10
13
16
19
```

The same code can be equivalently written using a while loop as follows.

```
i = 10
while i < 20:
print(i)
i = i + 3
```

Unlike the while loop, since the for loop iterates through a finite sequence, we do not have to often worry about the termination condition.

**Example:** Print the negative numbers from a given sequence.

We can use a for loop to go over a given sequence and print the number if it is negative.

```
numbers = [65, 32, -3, 32, 43, 32, -22, 2, -5, -7, 0, -9]
for n in numbers:
if n < 0:
print(n)
```

**Example:** Find the continent with the longest name.

We can store the continents in a list and iterate through them using a for loop. To find the length of a string, we can use the len() function. Finding the maximum length requires maintaining a maxlen variable. However, to print the continent with the maximum length, we also need to store it in the maxcont variable – whenever we update maxlen. The corresponding code is below.

```
continents = ["Africa", "Antarctica", "Asia", "Australia", "Europe", "North America", "South America"]
maxlen = 0                # this initialization is important

for cont in continents:
if   maxlen < len(cont):
     maxlen = len(cont)
     maxcont = cont

print(maxcont)
```

Since there are two answers to this question, think about what would our code output. If we want the other answer to be output, what small change would you make to the code?

**Example:** Check if a given number is prime. The number is larger than 2.

We will use a simple algorithm which checks divisibility of a given number n with numbers from 2 to square root of n. sqrt() is a function for finding the square root defined in a module named math. For this, we will have to tell the Python interpreter that we want to use this module. This is done using an import statement.

```
import math, sys

n = int(input())

for i in range(2, 1 + int(math.sqrt(n))):     # note 1 + ...
if n % i == 0:                                # if i divides n
   print('Composite')
   sys.exit()

print('Prime')
```

The above program works for a number larger than 2. Line 1 imports math and sys modules. The former is for sqrt function (Line 5) while the latter is for exit function (Line 8), which terminates the program. The loop goes over all the integers from 2 to sqrt(n) and if any of them divides n (Line 6), then the number is not prime. What happens if we comment out Line 8?

**Future Connect:** We will learn about modules in a later unit. Consider a module to be a library of useful functions related to a specific domain.

In the above program, only 2 is an even divisor which needs to be checked, but we are unnecessarily checking against 4, 6, 8, … This can be easily avoided as follows.

```
1.  import math, sys
2.
3.  n = int(input())
4.
5.  if n % 2 == 0:
6.      print('Composite')
7.      sys.exit()
8.
9.  for i in range(3, 1 + int(math.sqrt(n)), 2):
10.     if n % i == 0:              # if i divides n
11.         print('Composite')
12.         sys.exit()
13.
14. print('Prime')
```

## Nested Loops and Loop Modifiers

Loops can be nested, that is, one loop can be inside another. Consider that we want to find all the prime numbers from 3 to 100. How can we modify the above program, which works for one number, to work for many numbers?

```
import math, sys

for n in range(3, 100+1):
print(n)
# code from the above program (Lines 5 – 14)
```

Unfortunately, the output of the above code consists of only two numbers.

```
3   Prime
4   Composite
```

This happens because we have sys.exit() after printing Composite. Exiting the program was okay for a single number, but not for a sequence of numbers. Ideally, we want that after finding out that a number is composite, we should not print Prime, but still go to the next number for primality checking.

Python provides loop modifiers to enable such a control-flow. The keyword break brings the control out of the currently enclosing nearest loop, while the keyword continue skips the rest of the iteration and goes to the next one. The whole program would now be as follows.

```
1.  import math
2.
3.  for n in range(3, 100+1):
4.      print(n)
5.
6.      if n % 2 == 0:
7.          print('Composite')
8.          continue                # go to the next number
9.
10. for i in range(3, 1 + int(math.sqrt(n)), 2):
11.     if n % i == 0:              # if i divides n
12.         print('Composite')
13.         break                   # come out of the loop at Line 10
14.
15.     print('Prime')
```

After Line 7 finds out that a number is even, Line 8 goes back to the next number in the range specified at Line 3, skipping Lines 9 – 15. Similarly, after finding a number composite at Line 12, Line 13 brings the control to Line 14, out of the for loop at Line 10. Note that Line 13 is enclosed in two loops (Line 3 and Line 10), but it comes out of the currently enclosing nearest loop, that is, Line 10's loop. The program now prints all the numbers from 3 to 100, and most of the outputs are correct, but some are wrong. For instance, the initial few lines are:

```
3   Prime
4   Composite
5   Prime
6   Composite
7   Prime
8   Composite
9   Composite Prime
10  Composite
    ...
```

Notice the output for number 9. Our code prints both Composite and Prime. Why does this happen? This is because break at Line 13 brings the control to Line 14. After that Line 15 continues to print Prime.

How do we correct this? We can keep track whether Composite was printed or not. If it was, then we need not print Prime; otherwise we should. The modified code looks like this.

```
import math

for n in range(3, 100+1):
    print(n, “, end=”)

    if n % 2 == 0:
        print(‘Composite’)
        continue                    # go to the next number

    composite = False

    for i in range(3, 1 + int(math.sqrt(n)), 2):
        if n % i == 0:              # if i divides n
            print(‘Composite’)
            composite = True
            break

    if composite == False:          # number is not composite
        print(‘Prime’)
```

The above code works well and produces the expected output.

**Future Connect:** Such a reuse of functionality (checking primality of one number) can be nicely encoded using functions. We can then call such a function in a loop.

Python provides a special construct to support the functionality we implemented using the variable composite. It is the else clause of a loop (for or while).

```
import math

for n in range(3, 100+1):
    print(n, “, end=”)

    if n % 2 == 0:
        print(‘Composite’)
        continue

    for i in range(3, 1 + int(math.sqrt(n)), 2):
        if n % i == 0:              # if i divides n
            print(‘Composite’)
            break
    else:                           # else corresponding to for
        print(‘Prime’)
```

Note the indentation of the else clause at Line 14. It corresponds to the for loop at Line 10 (and not to the if statement at Line 11). The else clause is executed if the loop exhausts all the elements in the sequence of numbers (or when the while condition becomes False), but does not get executed if the loop gets terminated by break. To understand this clause better, let's look at the following simple example.

```
for i in range(1, 10):
    print(i)
else:
    print("End:", i)

i = 1
while i < 10:
    print(i)
    i = i + 1
else:
    print("End:", i)
```

Can you analyze the program and find out the output of the above code? It is as below.

```
1
2
3
4
5
6
7
8
9
End: 9
1
2
3
4
5
6
7
8
9
End: 10
```

Note how the while loop increments the variable to 10, whereas the for loop retains its value to 9 at the end.

To understand the use of break and continue, let's consider the following example.

**Example:** Given a list, print all the positive numbers, but stop as soon as 0 is reached.

For instance, if the input list is [–4, 2, 54, 21, –32, 3, 6, 3, 1, 0, –5, 321], the output should print the values 2, 54, 21, 3, 6, 3, 1. It should not print 321. The program is as below.

```
numbers = [–4, 2, 54, 21, –32, 3, 6, 3, 1, 0, –5, 321]

for n in numbers:
    if n == 0:            # 0 is seen, come out of the loop
        break

    if n < 0:
        continue          # do not print negative numbers
    print(n)
```

Python also supports a pass statement, which can be used when no processing is required.

For instance, consider a *program where we wish to find the sum of* positive integers in a list which may contain negative numbers also.

```
numbers = [-4, 2, 54, 21, -32, 3, 6, 3, 1, 0, -5, 321]
sumn = 0

for n in numbers:
    if n < 0:
        pass
    else
        sumn = sumn + n

print(sumn)
```

Of course, the program can be modified to not require pass. But sometimes, it can be useful for readability purposes.

**Example:** Find birthdays in a month.

Say, you have friends whose birthdays are written in DD/MM/YY format. You want to find who all have birthdays in the month of August. To store birthdays, we can use key-value pairs, where name is the key and value is the birthdate. We will use the string index range to extract the MM part of the date.

```
birthdays = {‘Amit’:’01/07/00’, ‘Karan’:’02/08/99’, ‘Joel’:’28/07/01’,
             ‘Sunita’:’15/06/99’, ‘Shyam’:’10/08/00’, ‘Sudhira’:’29/02/00’}

for name, bday in birthdays.items():
    if bday[3:5] == ‘08’:            # August
        print(name)
```

The program stores names and birthdays in a dictionary (Lines 1 and 2). It then iterates through the key-value pairs using items() function (Line 4). It checks if the month is eighth, and if so, prints the name of the friend.

**Example:** Do you have the exact change?

You are given an infinite supply of notes of three denominations (say, 10 rupee, 20 rupee, and 50 rupee notes). Given a price, can you identify if you have exact change summing up to that price? For instance, using these three types of notes, we can pay 10, 20, 30, 40, 50, 60, 70 rupees, etc., but we cannot pay 55. It is also possible that the same price can be constructed using multiple combinations of notes. For instance, 50 rupees can be constructed using three notes of 10 and one note of 20, or by directly using a single 50 rupee note. We can print all the possible combinations. Consider the following sample inputs and outputs.

| Input | Output |
|---|---|
| 55<br>10 20 50 | No |
| 18<br>7 11 13 | 1 1 0 |
| 550<br>10 20 100 | 1 2 5<br>1 7 4<br>1 12 3<br>... |

A simple way to achieve this is by having a triply-nested loop going over various numbers of notes, and then checking every combination of notes. But since you have an infinite number of notes (as far as this example is concerned), when should individual loops terminate? The input price can help set the upper bound. The complete program is as below.

```
1.  price = int(input(‘Price: ’))
2.  deno1, deno2, deno3 = map(int, input(‘Denominations: ’).split())
3.
4.  print(“Can you form”, price, “exactly using”, deno1, deno2, deno3, “?”)
5.
6.  for d1 in range(0, 1 + price // deno1):
7.      for d2 in range(0, 1 + price // deno2):
8.          for d3 in range(0, 1 + price // deno3):
9.              if d1 * deno1 + d2 * deno2 + d3 * deno3 == price:
10.                 print(d1, d2, d3)
11. else:
12.     print(‘No’)
```

Line 2 uses the split() function to receive three fields (strings). To map those to integers, we can use the map() function. Lines 6–8 run a triply-nested loop which check all possible combinations of the three denominations, upper bounding by the price. For instance, if the price is 550, there is no point in using more than five 100-rupee notes. If such an exact combination is found, we print it at Line 10. If no such combination exists, then we print No at Line 12 (Line 11 is an else corresponding to the outermost for loop).

## UNIT SUMMARY

We explored various basic control constructs in Python such as conditionals and loops. We solved various problems using those constructs. We also looked at various loop modifiers which allow special control flow.

## EXERCISES

### Multiple Choice Questions

1. What is the output of the following program for the input 100 99?

```
n1, n2 = input().split()
if n1 < n2:
  print(n1, "<", n2)
elif n1 == n2:
  print(n1, "==", n2)
elif n1 < n2:
  print(n1, "again <", n2)
else:
  print(n1, ">=", n2)
```

(a) 100 < 99 (b) 100 >= 99 (c) 100 == 99 (d) 100 again < 99

2. Suggest a value for the dob variable that illustrates usefulness of short-circuiting for the following conditional statement.

```
if len(dob) >= 5 and dob[3:5] == "08":
  print("You are an August person.")
```

(a) '29/10/1999' (b) '29/08/2000'
(c) '1/1/2001' (d) '123'

3. What is the output of the following program?

```
numbers = [65, 32, -3, 32, 43, 32, -22, 2, -5, 64, 0, 8]
i = 0
for n in numbers:
  if 2**i == n:
    print(n)
  i = i + 1
```

(a) 32 32 64 8 (b) 32 64 8 (c) 32 64 (d) 32

4. What should be the value of the expression X in the following program to print all the squares between 3 and 99?

```
import math
for n in range(3, 100):
    for i in range(2, int(math.sqrt(n)) + 1):
        if X:
            print(n)
```

(a) i + 1 == n
(b) i * i == n
(c) sqrt(n) * sqrt(n) == i
(d) n * n == i * i

5. What does the following program print?

```
n = int(input())
sumf = 0
for i in range(0, n):
    for j in range(0, n):
        if i * j == n:
            break
    else:
        continue
    sumf = sumf + i
print(sumf)
```

(a) Sum of all the proper factors of n
(b) Sum of all the prime factors of n
(c) Sum of all the numbers smaller than n
(d) Sum of all the factors that are square roots

| ANSWERS | | | | | | | | | |
|---|---|---|---|---|---|---|---|---|---|
| 1. | (a) | 2. | (d) | 3. | (d) | 4. | (b) | 5. | (a) |

## PRACTICAL

1. Write a program to find the second maximum in a list.
2. Implement Python's exponentiation operator (**).
3. Modify our denominations program to support a fixed number of notes for each denomination.
4. Given name to state mapping of your friends, find all the friends from Telangana.
5. Given a number, find all its unique prime factors.

## Dynamic QR Code for Further Reading

# 3 Functions, Modules and Packages

## UNIT SPECIFICS

Through this unit we discuss the following aspects:

- Separating a functionality using functions
- Grouping functions using modules
- Grouping modules using packages

## RATIONALE

Good programming demands grouping coherent statements that solve a given problem. This grouping makes the calling code free of internal details, and also makes the code readable. This modularization is achieved at different levels in Python. Grouping of statements together is done using functions. Functions related to a particular domain are grouped into modules. Finally, modules can be clubbed together into a full-fledged package. We uncover this three-level hierarchy in this unit by creating our own functions, modules, and packages.

## PRE-REQUISITE

Unit 1 and 2

## UNIT OUTCOMES

List of outcomes of this unit is as follows:

**U3-O1:** Create new functions and call them

**U3-O2:** Create new modules and use them

**U3-O3:** Create new packages from the modules

| Unit-3 Outcomes | EXPECTED MAPPING WITH COURSE OUTCOMES (1- Weak Correlation; 2- Medium correlation; 3- Strong Correlation) | | | | | |
|---|---|---|---|---|---|---|
| | CO-1 | CO-2 | CO-3 | CO-4 | CO-5 | CO-6 |
| U3-O1 | 3 | 3 | 3 | – | 3 | 1 |
| U3-O2 | 1 | 1 | 2 | 2 | 1 | – |
| U3-O3 | 2 | 1 | 3 | 1 | 2 | 1 |

As code sizes grow and we work on larger projects, it is imperative to organize our code. We start this unit with a block diagram depicting the relationship between functions, modules, and packages. We then delve deeper into each of them.

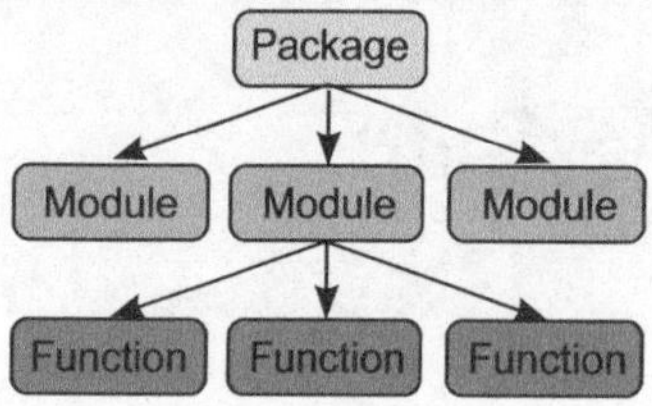


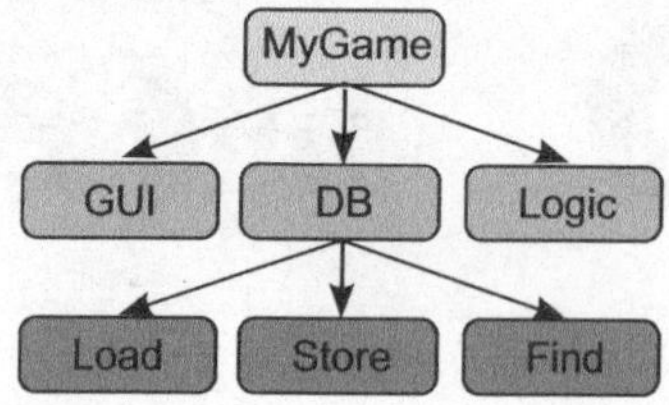


The above diagram shows the hierarchy. A package may contain multiple modules and each module may contain multiple functions. For instance, if we are designing a game, within the package MyGame, we can have different modules which deal with the graphical user interface (GUI), or database (DB), or the logic of the game. Within each module, we may group related functions. For instance, a DB module may have to load data from a database (which may be a relational database such as SQL or using files on disk), store the current game and scores in the database, and find information about a user in it. We will explore this hierarchy bottom up.

## 3.1 FUNCTIONS

Functions allow us to separate a specific functionality and reuse it from multiple places. For instance, we use the functions print and len() which are defined in the standard Python library. But we can write our own functions too!

Let's begin with defining a function for printing a message and calling it in different ways.

```
1.  def hello():                # function definition
2.      print("Hello World!")
3.
4.  hello()                     # function call
5.
6.  if False:
7.      hello()                 # function call inside a conditional
8.
9.  for i in range(1, 3):
10.     hello()                 # function call inside a loop
```

Lines 1 – 2 define a new function hello() using def keyword. Simply defining a function does not execute it. We need to call it explicitly, which we do at Line 4. Functions can be called from other control constructs too: for instance, from a conditional at Line 7 and from a loop at Line 10. The output of the whole program is three instances of "Hello World!", one from Line 4, none from Line 7, and two from Line 10. The main module (Lines 3 – 10) from where we call a function is called a caller.

Let us now modify our hello()'s definition to support different messages being printed. This demands an argument.

```
def hello(msg):
    print(msg)

hello("Hello World!")

if False:
    hello("Hello from if")

for i in range(1, 3):
    hello("Hello from loop")
```

The output of the above code is:

```
Hello World!
Hello from loop
Hello from loop
```

Such arguments can help tune the functionality. This is what we do with a print() function.

Recall our program from Unit 2 which found out if a range of numbers is prime or not. We will modify it to use functions and see how the program looks simplified.

**Example:** Find out if numbers from 3-to-100 are prime, using functions.

Here is the original program without using functions.

```
1.  import math
2.
3.  for n in range(3, 100+1):
4.      print(n, '', end='')
5.
6.      if n % 2 == 0:
7.          print('Composite')
8.          continue
9.
10.     for i in range(3, 1 + int(math.sqrt(n)), 2):
11.         if n % i == 0:          # if i divides n
12.             print('Composite')
13.             break
14.     else:                       # else corresponding to for
15.         print('Prime')
```

Which part can we move to a function? That is up to us. For instance, we can simply make printing Prime or Composite inside a function. Alternatively, we can convert the for loop at Line 12 into a function. From the perspective of this example, we can make primality testing of a given number as a function. This function can then be called from the loop at Line 3.

```
1.  import math
2.
3.  def isPrime(n):
4.      if n % 2 == 0:
5.          print(‘Composite’)
6.          continue                    # there is no enclosing loop
7.
8.      for i in range(3, 1 + int(math.sqrt(n)), 2):
9.          if n % i == 0:              # if i divides n
10.             print(‘Composite’)
11.             break
12.     else:                           # else corresponding to for
13.         print(‘Prime’)
14.
15. for n in range(3, 100+1):
16.     print(n, ‘’, end=’’)
17.     isPrime(n)
```

See how we have moved the code to the isPrime() function and the main module is simplified (Lines 15 – 17). Unfortunately, this code reorganization poses an issue. The continue statement at Line 6 is now no longer inside a loop. Hence, it is a syntax error. From the perspective of a function, we want that after printing Composite at Line 5, the control should go back to the caller and the next number should be checked for primarily. This can be done using a return statement.

6. return

Now the program works as expected. It will be nice however, if the caller can take charge of the processing after finding if a number is prime or not. This demands the function isPrime() to return True or False.

```
import math

def isPrime(n):
    if n % 2 == 0:
        return False

    for i in range(3, 1 + int(math.sqrt(n)), 2):
        if n % i == 0:
            return False
    else:
        return True

for n in range(3, 100+1):
    if isPrime(n): print(n, end=’, ’)
```

Lines 5, 9, and 11 return a boolean value depending upon the argument number's primality. If the number is composite, the caller does not do anything, otherwise it prints the number. The output of the above code is:

```
3, 5, 7, 11, 13, 17, 19, 23, 29, 31, 37, 41, 43, 47, 53, 59, 61, 67, 71, 73, 79, 83, 89, 97,
```

Do we need to always make 100 calls to get these prime numbers? Not necessarily. We can invoke a function only once and return a full list of primes! Let's do it. This will require us to push the for loop inside the function.

```
1.  import math
2.
3.  def getAllPrimes(maxn):          # find primes upto maxn
4.      allPrimes = []
5.
6.      for n in range(3, maxn+1):
7.          if n % 2 == 0:
8.              continue                # we can use this now
9.
10.         for i in range(3, 1 + int(math.sqrt(n)), 2):
11.             if n % i == 0:
12.                 break
13.         else:
14.             allPrimes.append(n)     # add to the list
15.
16.     return allPrimes
17.
18. # main module begins here
19. print(getAllPrimes(100))
20. print(getAllPrimes(50))
```

The argument to the function is now the maximum number up to which we wish to check primality. We store all such primes into a list allPrimes initialized in Line 4. As soon as we find a prime number (Line 13), we push it to this list (Line 14). This populated list is finally returned from the function (Line 16). Lines 19 and 20 call the function with different maxn values, and print the lists as below.

```
[3, 5, 7, 11, 13, 17, 19, 23, 29, 31, 37, 41, 43, 47, 53, 59, 61, 67, 71, 73, 79, 83, 89, 97]
[3, 5, 7, 11, 13, 17, 19, 23, 29, 31, 37, 41, 43, 47]
```

## Global Variables

In the above example, the list was defined inside the function and returned to the caller. We can as well define the list outside the function, populate it inside the function, and print the populated list from the main module (without the function returning it). This requires the list to be defined globally.

```
1. import math
2.
3. def getAllPrimes(maxn):                  # find primes upto maxn
4.     global allPrimes                     # I want to access allPrimes list
5.
6.     for n in range(3, maxn+1):
7.         if n % 2 == 0:
8.             continue                     # we can use this now
9.
10.        for i in range(3, 1 + int(math.sqrt(n)), 2):
11.            if n % i == 0:
12.                break
13.        else:
14.            allPrimes.append(n)          # add to the list
15.
16. # main module begins here
17. allPrimes = []
18. getAllPrimes(100)                       # populate allPrimes
19. print(allPrimes)
20. getAllPrimes(50)                        # populate allPrimes
21. print(allPrimes)
```

The function getAllPrimes() remains almost the same, except for two changes. One: at Line 4, it marks allPrimes to be a global variable. Two: it does not (need to) return allPrimes. allPrimes is now a regular variable in the main module initialized to an empty list at Line 17. It is populated by getAllPrimes() at Lines 18 and 20. Note that after these two function calls, we simply print allPrimes list in Lines 19 and 21. What will be the output of the code?

If you said that the output will remain the same, that is not correct. Here is the output.

```
[3, 5, 7, 11, 13, 17, 19, 23, 29, 31, 37, 41, 43, 47, 53, 59, 61, 67, 71, 73, 79, 83, 89, 97]
[3, 5, 7, 11, 13, 17, 19, 23, 29, 31, 37, 41, 43, 47, 53, 59, 61, 67, 71, 73, 79, 83, 89, 97, 3, 5, 7, 11, 13,
17, 19, 23, 29, 31, 37, 41, 43, 47]
```

Note how the second call to getAllPrimes() has appended the prime numbers to the original list. This happened because we forgot to initialize the list to empty before calling getAllPrimes(50) at Line 20.

**Remember:** Global variables make the code easy, but can also lead to initialization errors if we are not careful.

To understand the scope of global variables, let's look at a simple example. What will be the output of this code?

```
1.  g = 10                  # global variable
2.  print(“1:”, g).
3.
4.  def fun():
5.      g = 20              # local variable
6.      print(“3:”, g)
7.
8.  g = 30                  # global variable
9.  print(“2:”, g)
10. fun()
11. print(“4:”, g)
```

A function can be defined in the middle of the main module (Line 4). The program works as follows.

Line 1: assigns 10 to a global variable g.

Line 2: prints 1: 10

Line 8: assigns 30 to the same global variable g.

Line 9: prints 2: 30

Line 10: makes a function call to fun() at Line 4.

Line 5: assigns 20 to a local variable g. This is a new variable, different from the global g.

Line 6: prints 3: 20

The control now comes back to the caller. The local variable is no longer accessible.

Line 11: prints 4: 30. This is the same earlier global variable g.

To summarize, when fun() accesses a variable, it is the local variable by default. If we want it to access the global variable g, we will have to add the statement: global g, similar to the last example (global allPrimes). Then the output will change to 4: 20.

**Good Programming Practice:** If there are central structures holding data which you need to access from several functions, then only use global variables. Otherwise, avoid globals and pass the data as arguments to functions.

**Example:** Perfect numbers.

A number is perfect if the sum of its proper divisors equals itself. For instance, 6 is a perfect number as its proper divisors (1, 2, 3) sum to 6. Another perfect number is 28 = 1 + 2 + 4 + 7 + 14. Let's write a program to find perfect numbers using functions.

The main module can be written as below.

```
for n in range(1, 10000):
    factors = findFactors(n)

    if n == sum(factors):
        print(n, “:”, factors)
```

We make use of two functions: findFactors and sum. The latter is a predefined function in Python, while we will have to write the former. With our experience of primality testing, we know how to write it.

```
def findFactors(n):
    factors = []

    for f in range(1, n):
        if n % f == 0:
            factors.append(f)

    return factors;
```

**Example:** Fibonacci strings

Like Fibonacci numbers, we can define Fibonacci strings, which are strings over binary digits 0 and 1.

Fib(0) = “0”, Fib(1) = “01”

Fib(n) = Fib(n – 1) + Fib(n – 2), where + is Python's string concatenation

A few initial Fibonacci strings are: 0, 01, 010, 01001, 01001010, 0100101001001, …

Fibonacci strings have a special property. If we remove the last two digits, then the string reads the same forward and backward. Such strings are called palindromes (e.g., nitin, a, malayalam, amma, tattarrattat, and if you permit spaces and punctuation, “borrow or rob”, “was it a car or a cat I saw?”, “never odd or even”, “A man, a plan, a canal – panama”).

Let's check if Fibonacci strings have this fascinating property.

```
def isPalindrome(bstring):
    blen = len(bstring)
    first = bstring[:blen // 2]             # integer division to get the index
    second = bstring[(blen + 1) // 2:]

    if first == second[::-1]:               # extended range, for reversing
        return True

    return False

# main module begins
first = “0”
second = “01”
i = 0

while i < 10:
    if i >= 2 and isPalindrome(first[:-2]):
        print(first[:-2] + “ is a palindrome”)

    first, second = second, second + first
    i = i + 1
```

We define the first two strings in Lines 12 and 13. We check this property for the first few Fibonacci strings (Line 16). The strings are generated in Line 20 using the multiple assignment form. Line 17 uses a conjunct to call function isPalindrome() by removing the last two binary digits of the eligible strings. If the property is satisfied, all the strings should get printed by Line 18.

The function isPalindrome() splits the given string into two halves. [0:blen // 2] is the first half, while the second half is [(blen + 1) // 2: blen], which we use in Lines 3 and 4. Interestingly, the expressions work whether the string is even length or odd. Note that we use the same variable names (first and second) in both the main module and the function, but both refer to two different entities. Line 6 uses a peculiar syntax [::-1] which defines a range, but also uses a step (-1 in this case, 1 by default) which allows us to reverse the string second. If the two strings are the same, we declare it to be a palindrome.

The output of the above code is:

```
0 is a palindrome
010 is a palindrome
010010 is a palindrome
01001010010 is a palindrome
0100101001001010010 is a palindrome
01001010010010100101001001010010 is a palindrome
01001010010010100101001001010010010100101001001010010 is a palindrome
010010100100101001010010010100100101001010010010100101001001010010100100101001001010010 is a palindrome
```

An interesting aspect of writing functions is that we can reuse it in different contexts. For instance, the isPalindrome() function works not only for binary strings, but also for arbitrary strings.

## Default Arguments

Consider a function wherein we need to initialize a sequence of integers. We need to know the size of the sequence expected and the value to which the sequence needs to be initialized. The function can be written as:

```
def initSeq(size, val):
    seq = []

    for i in range(0, size):
        seq.append(val)

    return seq
```

The function can be called as:

```
initSeq(10, 0)
initSeq(100, "ABCD")
initSeq(1000, ['A', 'B', 'C', 'D'])
```

This is good, since the same function can be used with multiple types of variables (integers, strings, lists), while the most common usage in an application could be integers. Also, the most common initialization may be to value 0. Can we avoid mentioning that?

Default arguments allow us to specify fewer arguments than what the function usually takes, and still achieve the desired (most common) functionality. Have we used such a feature before? We did. Recall that print() function takes optional arguments for sep and end. They default to the most common values of space and newline. We would like to do something similar with our initSeq(). We would like to call it as initSeq(10) and it should return a sequence of 10 zeros. Zero should be the default value.

Our program with default arguments looks as below.

```
1.  def initSeq(size, val = 0):
2.      seq = []
3.
4.      for i in range(size):
5.          seq.append(val)
6.
7.      return seq
```

Note how we specified assignment to val at Line 1. That is the default value when unspecified. How do we unspecify a value? By calling the function as: initSeq(10), without mentioning the initialization value. Thus, the following two calls are equivalent.

initSeq(10, 0)

initSeq(10)

Default arguments can come in handy for incremental software development while supporting backward compatibility. For instance, let's say that we have been asked to extend the functionality of initSeq() to include support for increasing sequences such as (0, 1, 2, 3, 4, 5, 6, 7, 8, 9). Note that our current code cannot create such a sequence. Now, if we add another argument, the existing callers using the original functionality would be affected – and their code will have to be rewritten. Can default arguments help us here?

```
def initSeq(size, val = 0, inc = 0):
    seq = []

    for i in range(size):
        seq.append(val)
        val = val + inc

    return seq

print(initSeq(10))
print(initSeq(9, 1))
print(initSeq(8, “1”, “0”))
print(initSeq(7, [‘A’, ‘B’, ‘C’], [‘D’]))
```

We define a second default argument inc (Line 1) and use it to update the value val (Line 6). Let's see how each of the calls to initSeq() work.

- Line 10 creates a sequence of 10 integers with value 0. The update from 0 to 0 in Line 6 is redundant but does not affect correctness. Thus, the original code continues to work as before.
- Line 11 also works as before, with the value set to 1 instead of the default zero.
- Line 12 is the new call using strings. It initializes a sequence of 8 binary strings representing powers of 2.
- Line 13 is the new call using lists. Can you find out what it does?

The output of the above program is:

```
[0, 0, 0, 0, 0, 0, 0, 0, 0, 0]
[1, 1, 1, 1, 1, 1, 1, 1, 1]
['1', '10', '100', '1000', '10000', '100000', '1000000', '10000000']
[['A', 'B', 'C'], ['A', 'B', 'C', 'D'], ['A', 'B', 'C', 'D', 'D'], ['A', 'B', 'C', 'D', 'D', 'D'], ['A', 'B', 'C', 'D', 'D', 'D',
'D'], ['A', 'B', 'C', 'D', 'D', 'D', 'D', 'D'], ['A', 'B', 'C', 'D', 'D', 'D', 'D', 'D', 'D']]
```

## Recursion

L. Peter Deutsch said: to iterate is human, to recurse, divine. Recursion is when a function calls itself (directly or indirectly). It may sound funny, but we use recursive formulation all the time. Recall our Fibonacci sequence Fib(n) = Fib(n – 1) + Fib(n – 2), or factorial Fact(n) = n * Fact(n – 1). In fact, some of the other computations could also be modeled using recursion. For instance, we can say that sum(list[:]) == list[0] + sum(list[1:]).

To start with, let's implement our initSeq() recursively. Note that currently it is implemented iteratively (using a for loop at Line 4). How should its recursive formulation be?

1. initSeq(size, val) = one element with val, followed by (size – 1) elements with val
   = [val] + initSeq(size – 1, val)
2. initSeq(0, val) = []

Equation 1 is the inductive step, while Equation 2 is the base case (which allows recursion to stop). Let's implement the function using our formulation.

```
1. def initSeq(size, val):
2.     if size == 0:                    # base case
3.         return []
4.
5.     return [val] + initSeq(size - 1, val)  # inductive step
```

Note the similarity between Equation 1 and Line 5 (also Equation 2 and Lines 2 – 3).

**Example:** Print a list recursively.

The recursive formulation for printing a list recursively is:

1. printrec(list) = print the first element, followed by printing the remaining elements
   = print(list[0])
   printrec(list[1:])

2. printrec([]) = pass

Let's implement the program as per this formulation.

```
1.  def printrec(mylist):
2.      if mylist == []:                    # base case
3.          print()
4.          return
5.
6.      print(mylist[0], ' ', end='')    # inductive step
7.      printrec(mylist[1:])
8.
9.  printrec([0, 1, 2, 3, 4])
10. printrec(["king,", "are", "you", "glad", "you", "are", "king?"])
```

The if condition at Line 2 implements the base case, while the processing at Lines 6 and 7 follows the recursive formulation in Equation 1 (the other arguments to print are for pretty-printing). The output of the program is as expected.

What if I want to print the list in reverse? What would be the recursive formulation? How would the program look like?

```
1.  def printrec(mylist):
2.      if mylist == []:                    # base case
3.          print()
4.          return
5.
6.      printrec(mylist[1:])
7.      print(mylist[0], ' ', end='')    # inductive step
8.
9.  printrec([0, 1, 2, 3, 4])
10. printrec(["king,", "are", "you", "glad", "you", "are", "king?"])
```

It turns out that simply by exchanging Lines 6 and 7, one can get the reversed list.

**Example:** Binary search

One of the classical search algorithms is binary search in a sorted array. We will assume ascending unique values, and implement this search recursively. The idea is to go to the middle of this sorted sequence, and check if the key is found. If yes, we return the index. Otherwise, we decide to recursively search either in the left or the right half.

Do we use binary search in real life?

- When a teacher asks you to go to page 140, do you flip through the first 139 pages?
- If we need to find the meaning of a word supercalifragilisticexpialidocious in a dictionary, how do we reach the word?
- If we want to search for the phone number of Star Garage in a directory, do we go sequentially?

The following example illustrates binary search. Consider the following sorted array of numbers, with our search key as 10. We first check the middle element (53). Since 10 is smaller than 53, we ignore the right half of 53 and choose to search in the first half (-4…50). The middle element of this sequence is 9, which is our second probe. Since our search key 10 is larger than 9, we choose to search on the right hand side of 9 (10..50). The middle element of this sequence is 11, which is our probe 3. Since our search key 10 is less than 11, we choose to search its left half (10..10). We finally find our search key.

| | | | ↓2 | ↓4 | ↓3 | | ↓1 | | | | | | | |
|---|---|---|---|---|---|---|---|---|---|---|---|---|---|---|
| –4 | 2 | 5 | 9 | 10 | 11 | 50 | 53 | 69 | 77 | 89 | 91 | 93 | 99 | 102 |

Two important differences between linear search and binary search are:

1. Linear search works with unsorted sequences also.
2. The number of probes a binary search performs is much smaller than that in linear search.

The program for binary search can be implemented as follows.

```
1.  l = [-4, 2, 5, 9, 10, 11, 50, 53, 69, 77, 89, 91, 93, 99, 102]   # must be sorted
2.
3.  def binarysearch(value, start, end):   # search for value in l[start:end]
4.      global l
5.
6.      if start < end:                    # while there is at least one element
7.          mid = (start + end) // 2
8.
9.          if l[mid] == value:            # found the element
10.             return mid
11.         elif l[mid] < value:           # go to the right half
12.             return binarysearch(value, mid + 1, end)
13.         else:                          # go to the left half
14.             return binarysearch(value, start, mid)
15.
16.     else:                              # did not find the key
17.         return -1
18.
19. print(binarysearch(10, 0, len(l)))     # 4
20. print(binarysearch(-4, 0, len(l)))     # 0
21. print(binarysearch(12, 0, len(l)))     # -1
22. print(binarysearch(92, 0, len(l)))     # -1
23. print(binarysearch(102, 0, len(l)))    # 14
24. print(binarysearch(111, 0, len(l)))    # -1
```

We make use of a global list (Lines 1 and 4). The search function is called with the start and the end indices, along with the key to search (Lines 19 – 24). The processing checks if there is at least one element in between the start index and the end index (Line 6). If there isn't, that means the key is not found and we return -1 (Line 17). Otherwise, we check the middle element of the sequence for the key (Line 9). If it is found, we return its index (Line 10). Otherwise, we decide to continue searching in the right (line 12) or the left half (Line 14).

## 3.2 MODULES

Modules are what we have been writing so far. Each program we have created is a module, just that we did not look at them that way. Typically, a module is a collection of cohesive functions. For instance, while designing a large application, we may want to keep all the functions related to database processing, frontend, error handling, utilities in different modules. Let's recall our prime number program. Say, we have stored it in a file primefun.py.

```
1.  import math                   # name of this file is primefun.py
2.
3.  def isPrime(n):
4.      if n % 2 == 0:
5.          return False
6.
7.      for i in range(3, 1 + int(math.sqrt(n)), 2):
8.          if n % i == 0:
9.              return False
10.     else:
11.         return True
12.
13. for n in range(3, 100+1):
14.     if isPrime(n): print(n, end=', ')
15. print()
```

We can now make use of this module from a different Python script or program. Let's define it in a file primefunmodule.py.

```
import primefun
```

Note that there is only one line in this file. We can now execute this script.

```
$ python3 primefunmodule
3, 5, 7, 11, 13, 17, 19, 23, 29, 31, 37, 41, 43, 47, 53, 59, 61, 67, 71, 73, 79, 83, 89, 97,
```

Where do we get this output from? From Lines 13 – 15 of primefun.py which is imported by primefunmodule.py. Typically, when we make use of modules, the module files have functions and global variables, and do not contain the executable code (such as Lines 13 – 15). Note that the module primefun itself imports another module called math (Line 1).

Let's make further use of the imported module.

```
1.  import primefun
2.
3.  for n in range(3, 50+1):
4.      if primefun.isPrime(n): print(n, end=', ')
5.  print()
```

Thus, we can call a function from a module using modulename.functionname syntax (Line 4). The output of the above code is:

```
3, 5, 7, 11, 13, 17, 19, 23, 29, 31, 37, 41, 43, 47, 53, 59, 61, 67, 71, 73, 79, 83, 89, 97,
3, 5, 7, 11, 13, 17, 19, 23, 29, 31, 37, 41, 43, 47,
```

Note that the first line is printed by the code in primefun.py, while the second one is by the code in primefunmodule.py. We can also rename an imported entity and can import everything from a module, so that we can directly make use of the functions and globals from that module (instead of using the syntax modulename.functionname).

```
1.  import primefun
2.
3.  for n in range(3, 50+1):
4.      if primefun.isPrime(n): print(n, end=', ')
5.  print()
6.
7.  myprime = primefun.isPrime       # shorthand name
8.
9.  if myprime(22): print(22)        # use the shorthand name
10. else: print("22 is composite")
11.
12. from primefun import *           # import everything from a module
13.
14. if isPrime(23): print(23)        # and use the function directly
15. else: print("23 is composite")
```

Line 7 creates a shorthand name (like a pointer) to our isPrime function, which we can use in Line 9. This avoids using primefun.isPrime() type syntax as in Line 4. another way to use the isPrime() function directly is by importing only the function isPrime from the module primefun or importing everything (indicated by *) as in Line 12, and then using the function in Line 14. The output of the above code is:

```
3, 5, 7, 11, 13, 17, 19, 23, 29, 31, 37, 41, 43, 47, 53, 59, 61, 67, 71, 73, 79, 83, 89, 97,
3, 5, 7, 11, 13, 17, 19, 23, 29, 31, 37, 41, 43, 47,
22 is composite
23
```

**Note:** You may see a directory named __pycache__ created when you use modules. Python precompiles the used modules and stores it in a binary form in this directory.

**Example:** Create a module to track academic performance.

Let's create an academics module which tracks the courses taken, their total credits, and earned points. We can also then provide a function to compute the CGPA. How do we store this information? For now, we will store it in associative sequences. For instance:

| Courses | CS1100 | CS1200 | AM1100 | ... |
|---|---|---|---|---|
| Credits | 9 | 12 | 9 | ... |
| Earned points | 10 | 9 | 9 | ... |

Thus, $i^{th}$ course has maximum credits of $i^{th}$ credits and our earned points are stored at the $i^{th}$ place. Thus, these three lists run in parallel.

What should be the functions supported in our academics module?

- Add a new course, along with its total credits and earned points.
- Drop a course (some courses are heavy).
- Print the whole academic record.
- Know the current CGPA = sum of (credits * points)/sum of credits

The above functions can be defined as follows.

```
def add(course, creditstotal, earnedpoints):
...
def drop(cc):
...
def cprint():
...
def cgpa():
...
```

Note that the lists are not passed as parameters. This means, we can keep those global.

A typical user of our module may use it as follows.

```
from academics import *
add("CS1100", 9, 10)
add("CS1200", 12, 9)
add("AM1100", 9, 9)
cprint()
print("1st Sem CGPA:", cgpa(), "\n")
add("EE2101", 12, 8)
add("CS2200", 12, 10)
drop("EE2101")
add("CS2310", 6, 10)
add("CS2710", 6, 9)
cprint()
print("2nd Sem CGPA:", cgpa(), "\n")
```

And a typical output is:

```
course credits earned
CS1100 9 10
CS1200 12 9
AM1100 9 9
1st Sem CGPA: 9.3
course credits earned
CS1100 9 10
CS1200 12 9
AM1100 9 9
CS2200 12 10
CS2310 6 10
CS2710 6 9
2nd Sem CGPA: 9.5
```

Without reading further, try writing your own academics module to support the above functionality. We now show the complete module.

```
courses = []
credits = []
earned  = []

def add(cc, cr, ea):
    courses.append(cc)
    credits.append(cr)
    earned.append(ea)

def drop(cc):
    index = courses.index(cc)       # find the index of cc
    #TODO: check if index is valid
    courses.pop(index)              # remove the element at index
    credits.pop(index)
    earned.pop(index)

def cprint():
    ii = 0
    print("course", "credits", "earned")

    for cc in courses:
        cr = credits[ii]
```

```
        ea = earned[ii]
        print(cc, cr, ea)
        ii = ii + 1

def cgpa():
    numerator = denominator = 0
    ii = 0

    for cr in credits:
        ea = earned[ii]
        numerator = numerator + cr * ea
        denominator = denominator + cr
        ii = ii + 1

    return numerator / denominator
```

One can enhance the above module in multiple ways, for instance, to print semester-wise SGPA, to support audit courses, etc.

**Future Connect:** We can store the academic information in a text file and read it from a Python program.

**Example:** Create a module for matrix operations.

Let's create a matrix module which can have some useful functions such as addition and multiplication. To initialize the matrix, let's add another function, and to test it, let's add a printing function too. The four function signatures would look like this:

```
def minit(rows, cols, val = 0, inc = 0):
...
def mprint(mat):
...
def madd(mat1, mat2):
...
def mmult(mat1, mat2):
...
```

How is a matrix represented? It can be a list of lists. For instance, [ [1, 2, 3], [4, 5, 6] ]. Before reading further, it would be helpful to try out writing the above four functions yourself.

Here is how we will be able to use it in a client program, assuming the above module is stored in matrix.py.

```
1.  from matrix import *
2.
3.  mat1 = minit(4, 4, 1, 0)
4.  mat2 = minit(4, 4, 10, 2)
5.  mprint(mat1)
6.  mprint(mat2)
7.
8.  mat3 = madd(mat1, mat2)
9.  mprint(mat3)
10.
11. mat4 = mmult(mat1, mat2)
12. mprint(mat4)
```

The output of the above program is:

```
1 1 1
1 1 1
1 1 1
10 12 14
16 18 20
22 24 26
11 13 15
17 19 21
23 25 27
48 54 60
48 54 60
48 54 60
```

The four matrices correspond to the four mprint statements in the program (Line 5 for mat1, Line 6 for mat2, Line 9 for mat3 which is addition of mat1 and mat2, while Line 12 for mat4 which is the multiplication of mat1 and mat2).

Let's now look at how to implement the four functions.

```
def minit(rows, cols, val = 0, inc = 0):        # using default arguments
mat = []

for i in range(rows):
mat.append([])                                  # create ith row

for j in range(cols):
mat[i].append(val)                              # create jth column
val = val + inc
```

```
return mat
def mprint(mat):
for i in range(len(mat)):
for j in range(len(mat[i])):
print(mat[i][j], ", end=")
print()                                    # newline after every row
print()                                    # newline after the matrix
def madd(mat1, mat2):
# TODO: check if their sizes are the same.
mat3 = []
for i in range(0, len(mat1)):
mat3.append([])
for j in range(len(mat1[i])):
mat3[i].append(mat1[i][j] + mat2[i][j])
return mat3
def mmult(mat1, mat2):
# TODO: check if cols of mat1 matches rows of mat2.
mat3 = []
for i in range(0, len(mat1)):
mat3.append([])
for j in range(len(mat2[0])):
psum = 0
for k in range(len(mat1[i])):        # triply nested loop
psum = psum + mat1[i][k] * mat2[k][j]
mat3[i].append(psum)
return mat3
```

The functions are self-explanatory, once you know what matrix addition and multiplication mean. The same library works with integers, reals, and complex numbers. For instance, we can use the module as follows.

```
mat1 = minit(4, 4, 1.2, 0)         # real numbers
mat2 = minit(4, 4, 10 + 4j, 2)     # complex numbers
mat3 = madd(mat1, mat2)
mat4 = mmult(mat1, mat2)
```

## 3.3 PACKAGES

A package encapsulates multiple modules of a project. From a data organization perspective, a module is stored in a .py file, while a package is the directory containing the .py file. We can then access a module mod in package pack as pack.mod. In general, a module file may not be directly inside a package directory, but may be nested deeper, due to multiple subdirectories – for instance, pack.subdir1.subdir2.mod. In such cases, each of subdir1, subdir2 etc. are called subpackages.

Let's consider a concrete example of a project. Say, we wish to implement a simple game – tic-tac-toe. A sample is shown below. In a 3 × 3 grid, two players fill in two symbols (say, X and O) in empty cells alternatively, and the first person getting three symbols in a row or a column or a diagonal wins. Sometimes, the game may end in a draw.

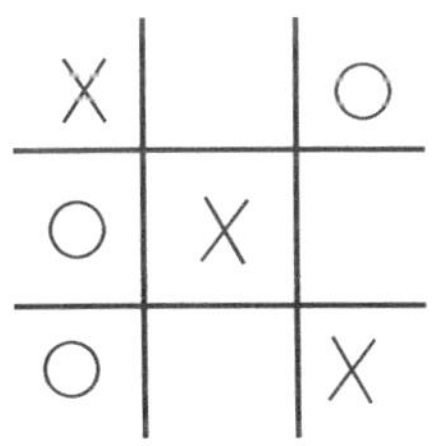

The game can be nicely implemented as a package, since it has multiple components. We need to have the game logic in one module, and game display in another. We can add more functionality such as storing the game in a file or storing the scores of the players which can be loaded from a database etc. But for now, we will constrain ourselves with two subpackages: logic and display. Within each of these subpackages, we may have multiple modules; for instance, text-based display and GUI-based display. The overall directory structure looks like this:

```
tictactoe/                  # package
|——__init__.py              # initializer
|——display                  # subpackage
| |——__init__.py            # initializer
| |——gui.py                 # GUI module
| |——text.py                # text module
|—— logic                   # subpackage
| |——__init__.py            # initializer
| |——twoplayer.py           # module
|——internal                 # regular directory, not a subpackage
```

The outermost directory represents the main package. Thus, if we have a user program using this package, say ttt.py, it will have the code as below.

```
import tictactoe
print("in ttt")
tictactoe.loadGame("text") # argument decides whether to load the game in text or GUI.
```

The package directory contains two subpackages: display and logic. It also contains a directory named internal, which can be used for internal bookkeeping. It is not a subpackage.

__init__.py is a special file of a package / subpackage which marks the enclosing directory as a package and initializes it. Without this file, the directory is not considered to be a package / subpackage (like internal directory). Thus, the code in __init__.py gets executed automatically when we import the corresponding package / subpackage. This can be useful to initialize our data structures etc. Thus, if we add appropriate print() statements to __init__.py files, we will see the following output before the game loads.

```
$ python3 ttt.py
in tictactoe/logic/init          # subpackage
in tictactoe/display/init        # subpackage
in tictactoe/init                # package
in ttt                           # application
```

Note how the initializations are happening. The innermost subpackages are initialized, and then the outer packages get initialized, only after which, the application begins. This happens because our tictactoe package also imports the internal subpackages, which executes the __init__.py files in those subdirectories.

While our code needs to use the fully qualified path package.subpack1.subpack2.variable, we can use shorthand idea to reduce the typing. For instance:

```
import tictactoe.logic
import tictactoe.display.text
board = tictactoe.logic.board              # shorthand data
show = tictactoe.display.text.show         # shorthand function
...
  if board[row][col] == symbol:
  ...
  show()                                   # same as tictactoe.display.text.show()
```

One thought that may occur here is whether we can use import *. By default, import * does not import everything from the package; it depends upon a variable called __all__ which needs to be defined in __init__.py, mentioning which subpackages to import. For instance, we can add the following in tictactoe/__init__.py:

```
__all__ = ["logic", "display"]
```

and can include further __all__ variables inside logic/__init__.py and display/__init__.py, only these subpackages are imported with import *. We should also note that typically, import * is not a good programming practice in the production environment, but can simplify fast prototyping. We avoid import * in our tictactoe code and use explicit fully-qualified names for the subpackages.

Since the logic of the overall game runs into multiple files spanning several lines, we will avoid showing the complete code here. You are encouraged to look at this book's webpage for the full code. But we will show you glimpses of the code's execution.

```
$ python3 ttt.py
in tictactoe/logic/init
in tictactoe/display/init
in tictactoe/init
in ttt
_ _ _
_ _ _
_ _ _
Player o: 0 0
o _ _
_ _ _
_ _ _

Player X: 1 1
o _ _
_ X _
_ _ _
Player o: 2 0
o _ _
_ X _
o _ _
Player X: 2 1
o _ _
_ X _
o X _
Player o: 1 0
o _ _
o X _
o X _
Player o wins.
```

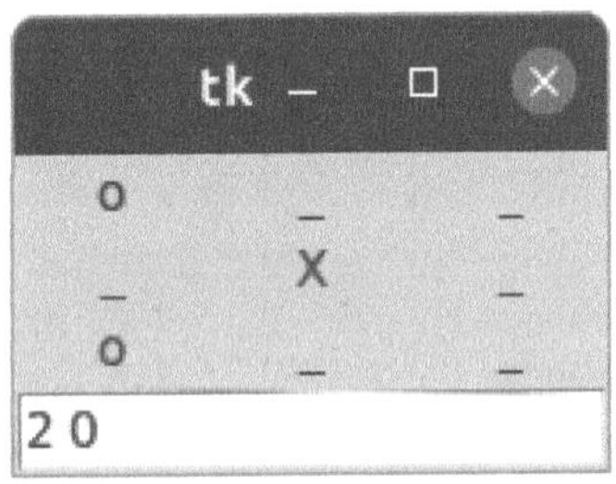


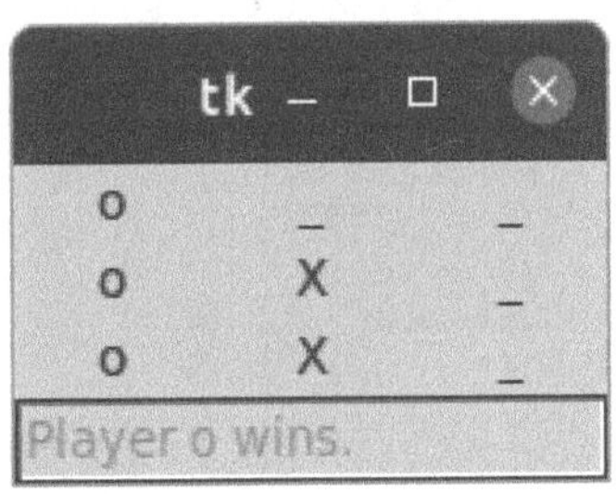


The left textbox shows text-based execution, while the right side screenshots show the GUI based execution of the same program – with the difference of tictactoe.loadGame("text") versus tictactoe.loadGame("gui"). Since the internal processing logic remains the same, we reuse that functionality, while changing only the display. The code can be enhanced in multiple ways, and we encourage the readers to try out the enhancements.

For convenience, we show the screenshots of the text and the gui based versions below.

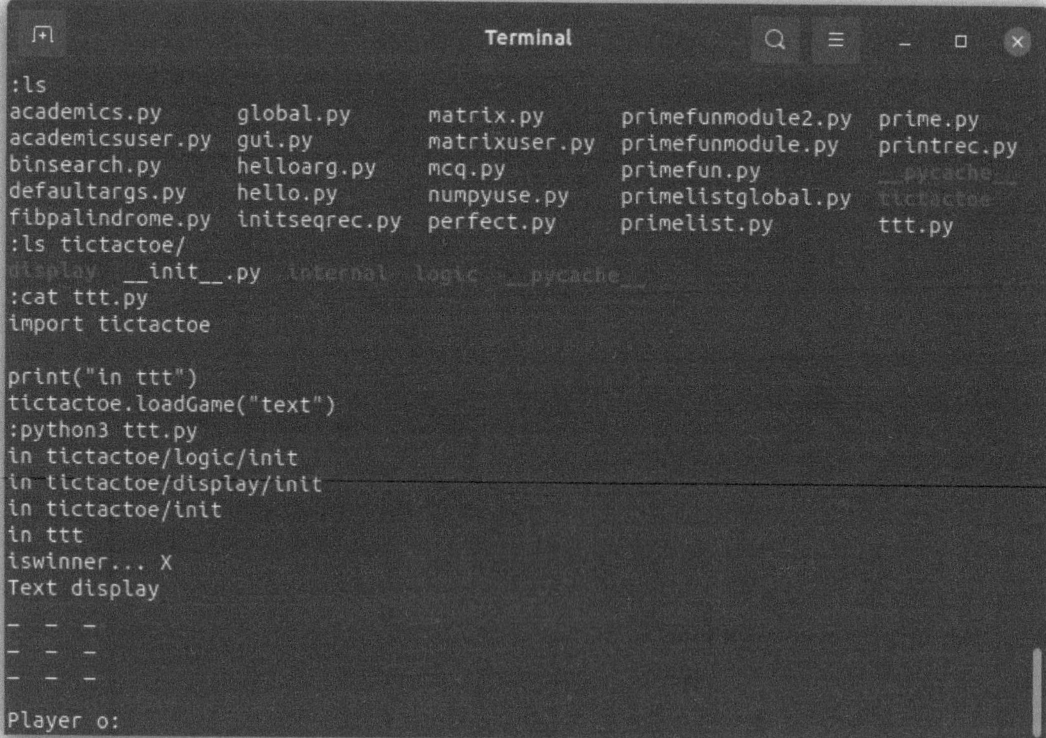


After changing ttt.py to load the gui, the screenshot is as below.

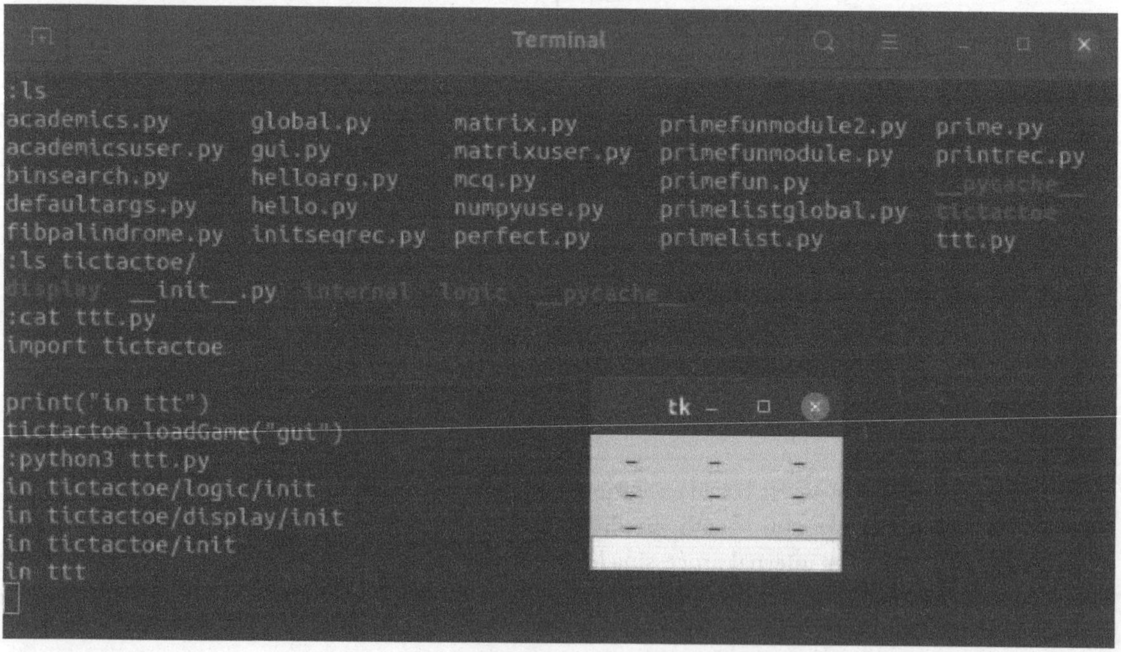

## UNIT SUMMARY

We learned various ways to group statements using functions, functions using modules, and modules using packages. In the process, we developed slightly larger codes which allow us to develop applications.

## EXERCISES

### Multiple Choice Questions

1. What is the output of the following program?

```
def swap(x, y):
    x, y = y, x
x, y = 1, 2
swap(x, y)
print(x, y)
```

(a) 1 2 (b) 2 1
(c) 1 1 (d) 2 2

2. What is the output of the following recursive code?

```
def rprint(l):
    if len(l) > 0:
        rprint(l[1:])
        print(l[0], end='')
rprint([1, 2, 3, 4, 5])
```

(a) 12345 (b) 2345
(c) 54321 (d) 5432

3. Consider the following code to compute the nth Fibonacci number.

```
def fib(n):
    if n < 2: return 1
    return fib(n - 1) + fib(n - 2)
```

If the function is invoked as fib(5), how many total invocations of the function fib() happen? That is, how many times, fib() gets called in total.

(a) 5 (b) 8
(c) 9 (d) 15

4. Consider a file dateutil.py which has useful functions such as today(), diff(date1, date2), etc. We want to use this function today() in our program written in file main.py in the same directory. How should this be done correctly?

(a) Import dateutil in main.py, and call dateutil.today().
(b) Since it is the same directory, we can directly call dateutil.today() without an import.
(c) Import dateutil in main.py, and call today().
(d) Directly call today() without an import.

5. Consider a package structure as below.

```
application/           # package
|—— __init__.py        # initializer
|—— display            # subpackage
| |—— __init__.py      # initializer
| |—— gui.py           # GUI module
| |—— text.py          # text module
|—— logic              # subpackage
| |—— __init__.py      # initializer
| |—— twoplayer.py     # module
|—— internal           # regular directory, not a subpackage
```

All the three __init__.py files (in application, display, and logic directories) are empty. A Python program using application has the following import statement:

```
import application
```

Which of the initializer files are executed due to the above import?
(a) None of the three
(b) __init__.py in application only
(c) __init__.py in application, display, and logic
(d) __init__.py in display and logic only

| ANSWERS | | | | | | | | | |
|---|---|---|---|---|---|---|---|---|---|
| 1. | (a) | 2. | (c) | 3. | (d) | 4. | (a) | 5. | (b) |

## PRACTICAL

1. Extend our *isPalindrome*() function to work with spaces and punctuation (e.g., "step on no pets!").
2. Enhance our academics module to support printing of semester-wise SGPA, apart from the cumulative CGPA. Further, support it for audit courses, which should be listed, but should not be counted towards CGPA.
3. Create a module to track your friends' information: name, phone number, date of birth, native city, website if any, instagram handle if exists. Now define various functions to add / modify / delete this information. Add further aggregate functionality, such as finding friends born in a given month, friends from a given city, etc.

4. Extend our tictactoe application to support taking input using mouse clicks (instead of row and column numbers). Further extend it for one-player game, that is, your program will be the second player.
5. Create a project for automation of one of the following: library, a general store, hotel room reservation, restaurant table booking. Design it as a package with appropriate subpackages and modules. If possible, work as a team so different students develop different subpackages. Ask one of your other friends to test its functionality.

## Dynamic QR Code for Further Reading

# 4 Files and Regular Expressions

## UNIT SPECIFICS

Through this unit we discuss the following aspects:

- Storing and retrieving data from files
- Text processing
- Pattern matching with regular expressions

## RATIONALE

If we want our data to be retained across multiple invocations of our Python programs, we will need to store it on a permanent storage such as disk. In this module we will study reading and writing files on the hard-disk. Further, we will also be able to use various string functions for processing text – which is a common scenario for using Python. Processing strings leads naturally to specifying a pattern, which can be succinctly described using regular expressions, which will be the last part of this unit.

## PRE-REQUISITE

Units 1 and 2

## UNIT OUTCOMES

List of outcomes of this unit is as follows:

**U4-O1:** Read an existing file and write to a file programmatically

**U4-O2:** Process text in various applications

**U4-O3:** Match a text with a given regular expression

| Unit-4 Outcomes | EXPECTED MAPPING WITH COURSE OUTCOMES (1- Weak Correlation; 2- Medium correlation; 3- Strong Correlation) | | | | | |
|---|---|---|---|---|---|---|
| | CO-1 | CO-2 | CO-3 | CO-4 | CO-5 | CO-6 |
| U4-O1 | 3 | 3 | 3 | – | 3 | 1 |
| U4-O2 | 1 | 1 | 2 | 2 | 1 | – |
| U4-O3 | 2 | 1 | 3 | 1 | 2 | 1 |

So far, whatever we stored in variables was unavailable after our Python program finished execution. In contrast, if you look at the Python program you wrote, you can see it in *file.py* file. What is the difference? Variables get stored in the computer's memory which is transient, whereas the program was stored in a file on disk, which is a permanent storage. Therefore, even if the computer reboots, the file continues to be available. We would like to access these files programmatically.

## 4.1 FILE INPUT/OUTPUT

In a Linux terminal, the command to print the contents of a file is cat, which can be used as follows:

```
$ ls                         # In Windows terminal: dir
hello.txt
$ cat hello.txt              # In Windows terminal: type
This is a text file.
It contains four lines.
The third line is empty.
```

Let's implement this functionality.

**Example:** Print contents of a file.

```
1. myfile = open('hello.txt')     # open the file for reading.
2.
3. for line in myfile:
4.     print(line)
5.
6. myfile.close()                 # close the file.
```

A file is opened for processing in Line 1 (the operating system sets up resources using which the file can be accessed), processed (Line 3), and closed in Line 6 (allowing the operating system to release the resources).

Can you guess the output of the above program? Well, it turns out to be more than what one may anticipate.

```
This is a text file.
It contains four lines.
The third line is empty.
```

This is because the file already contains a newline after every line, and print() adds another. We know how to fix it though (try it out).

It would be nice if we can provide the filename (hello.txt) on the command-line, instead of hardcoding in the program or prompting the user every time.

```
$ python3 cat.py hello.txt
This is a text file.
It contains four lines.
The third line is empty.
```

For accessing command-line arguments, we can use sys.argv. This variable is a list of arguments we provide while invoking the Python interpreter. Thus, argv[0] is "cat.py" and argv[1] is "hello.txt".

```
import sys

myfile = open(sys.argv[1])      # argv[1] contains the second argument

for line in myfile:
    print(line, end=”)

myfile.close()
```

We can use this new program on other text files too. For instance:

```
$ python3 cat.py ../unit1/power.py             # our program using ** operator
print(5 + 3 / 4 - 2)
print(3.1*3.2**3.3)
print(1234%10)
```

Note that since power.py is in another directory, we have provided a relative path.

**Example:** Copy a file.

We would like to make a copy of a file. Thus, the contents of the two files should be the same after running our Python program. We would like to execute it as follows:

```
$ ls
cat.py  cp.py  hello.txt                        # initially there are three files.
$ python3 cat.py hello.txt
This is a text file.
It contains four lines.
The third line is empty.
$ python3 cp.py hello.txt hellodup.txt          # copies file, does not print anything
$ ls
cat.py  cp.py  hello.txt  hellodup.txt          # now there are four.
$ python3 cat.py hellodup.txt
This is a text file.
It contains four lines.
The third line is empty.
```

We know how to read a file and use command-line arguments. But we don't know how to write to a file. It needs a second argument to the open() function.

**Past Connect:** Second argument can be made optional using default arguments.

```
import sys

infile = open(sys.argv[1] , ‘r’)            # open for reading
outfile = open(sys.argv[2] , ‘w’)           # open for writing

for line in infile:                         # read
    print(line, file=outfile, end=”)         # write

infile.close()
outfile.close()
```

You must have guessed why we named our program as cp.py. Linux has a command by that name to copy files.

**Example:** Split text into words.

We are given a text file textin.txt having the following contents.

```
Lexical analyzer groups a sequence of characters into tokens.
Syntax analyzer checks if these tokens adhere to a grammar syntax.
```

We would like to split it into words, and store it in another file textout.txt, as follows.

```
1: Lexical
2: analyzer
3: groups
4: a
5: sequence
6: of
7: characters
8: into
9: tokens.
10: Syntax
11: analyzer
12: checks
13: if
14: these
15: tokens
16: adhere
17: to
18: a
19: grammar
20: syntax.
```

We would like to invoke our program as follows.

```
$ python3 file-split.py textin.txt textout.txt
```

How do we write such a program? First, we need to utilize reading and writing of files and handling command-line arguments, as we just did. Apart from that, we need string processing to split a line into words using space as a separator. To print the word number, we need an iterative way to go over the words of a line.

```
1.  import sys
2.
3.  infile = open(sys.argv[1] , ‘r’)          # textin.txt
4.  outfile = open(sys.argv[2] , ‘w’)         # textout.txt
5.  ii = 1                                    # word number
6.
7.  for line in infile:
8.      words = line.split()
9.
10.     for ww in words:
11.         print(ii, ww, file=outfile, sep=’: ‘)
12.         ii = ii + 1                       # word number update
13.
14. infile.close()
15. outfile.close()
```

Note the similarity in Lines 7 and 10. The former goes over all the lines of a file, while the latter goes over all the words in a sequence of words. The function split() on Line 8 creates a word-sequence out of a string.

You can see that writing such simple utilities is not difficult in Python. Once you know how to do it, it is a matter of finding the right functions. Of course, writing programs in the best possible way requires a significant amount of practice.

**Example:** Join words to form sentences.

Let's now do the opposite of what we just did. Given a file textout.txt, containing a word per line preceded by the word number, can we generate back (almost) the original file textin.txt?

Such a processing requires us file handling similar to the previous example, except for the roles of the two files reversed for reading and writing. Apart from that, we need to separate out each word from the number, concatenate all the words, except when full-stop appears. Separating a word from its number can be done in multiple ways, one of them is using split(), and strings can be concatenated using + operator. How do we check if a string contains a full-stop?

```
1.  import sys
2.
3.  infile = open(sys.argv[1] , 'r')
4.  outfile = open(sys.argv[2] , 'w')
5.
6.  outline = ''                             # empty string
7.
8.  for line in infile:
9.      words = line.strip().split(': ')
10.     outline = outline + words[1] + " "     # one line, operator + joins strings
11.
12.     if "." in words[1]:                  # found the full-stop
13.         print(outline, file=outfile)
14.         outline = ''
15.
16. infile.close()
17. outfile.close()
```

The loop at Line 8 goes over all the lines in the input file. Each line (containing the number and the word) also contains a newline, which we remove using a function strip(). The function also removes any preceding spaces and tabs (which we do not have in our file). We then separate the number and the word using split(). Note how the output of strip() acts as an input to split(). After splitting, the word is stored in words[1], which we use in Line 12. Note the syntax of checking if a substring exists in a larger string.

**Discussion:** The reversal of the output is not perfect. If a line contains a dot in the middle, our program will split it in multiple sentences (e.g., cse.iitm.ac.in will follow a newline). We can modify the program to check if a word ends in a dot. But there will be words which will cause issues (e.g., e.g. this line.).

Simultaneous reading and writing

It is also possible to read a file and write to it while the file is open. We need to convey our intent a priori to the Operating System that we wish to open the file for both reading and writing. We illustrate this with an example.

**Example:** Replace all the occurrences of a word 'mispelt' in a file with 'misspelt'.

This simple utility teaches us several aspects of file handling. The given problem can be solved in multiple ways. But first look at a way which does not work.

```
import sys

myfile = open(sys.argv[1], 'r+')     # read + write

for line in myfile:
    modline = line.replace('mispelt', 'misspelt')
    print(modline, file=myfile, end='')

myfile.close()
```

Let's understand this erroneous code. We open the file in read-write mode in Line 3 (r+ conveys read-write mode). We then go over each line as before (Line 5), and replace all the occurrences of a word in that line with another and store the modified line in the modline variable (Line 6). We write this modified string to the file (Line 7).

For the following text in the input file:

```
If a word is mispelt it will be corrected.
This is the second line, which also contains mispelt word.
This is the third line.
```

the modified file is:

```
If a word is mispelt it will be corrected.
This is the second line, which also contains mispelt word.
This is the third line.
If a word is misspelt it will be corrected.
```

Without reading further, try to reason out why this can happen. Also, you are highly encouraged to try out whether you observe a similar behavior on your machine.

To understand this peculiar behavior, we need to first know that file input / output is buffered. This means, the operating system is not going to read the file on disk byte-by-byte, but as a large chunk. This chunk is copied to a buffer, which essentially is an array having a fixed size. How much buffer we have read or written is tracked using a pointer (or an array offset). Therefore, when we read / write a line in a file, this pointer, which is often called a file pointer, moves ahead. As long as the operation is getting done inside this buffer, further disk processing is avoided (because disk access is costlier than accessing this buffer in memory). If we end up reading beyond this buffer, the next part of the data is brought from the disk into another buffer and this process continues. The operating system also knows the size of the file. So it does not allow reading beyond the current file size.

Now let's come back and analyze the output of the above erroneous program. Due to Line 5, the operating system has already read the three lines into its buffer (including the newline characters). This buffer is processed line-by-line when we only read from the file. But because we also write in Line 7, it ends up writing at the end of the file (since the three lines have already been read). This adds the fourth line in the modified file and the file size increases. But where does the file pointer point due to this writing? It is at the end of the fourth sentence, which is the end of the file. Therefore, the next iteration of the for loop does not take place (you can check that by printing a message in the loop) and the loop gets over. The modified file is closed at Line 9 (which makes the operating system dump the modified buffer to the file on disk, if not done already).

How do we fix this? Clearly, to modify a word we have already read, the file pointer needs to go back in the file and rewrite that word. This is done using a function called seek(). So our second attempt is to use it to move the file pointer.

```
1.  import sys
2.
3.  myfile = open(sys.argv[1], ‘r+’)
4.
5.  for line in myfile:
6.      modline = line.replace(‘mispelt’, ‘misspelt’)
7.      curoff = myfile.tell()               # current file pointer
8.      myfile.seek(curoff - len(line))       # go back
9.      print(modline, file=myfile, end=”)
10.
11. myfile.close()
```

Line 7 gets the current file pointer (it is the number of bytes from the start of the file). We then try to go back to its position prior to reading the line using seek() (Line 8) and then write the modified line there (Line 9), attempting to overwrite the previously read line.

While our new processing at Lines 7 and 8 is useful, it is not permitted with such whole-file iteration (Line 5). The Python interpreter flags the following error:

```
Traceback (most recent call last):
  File "textcorrect.py", line 7, in <module>
            curoff = myfile.tell()
OSError: telling position disabled by next() call
```

To counter this, we will need to explicitly read a line from the file. This is done using the readline() function.

```
import sys

myfile = open(sys.argv[1], ‘r+’)
line = myfile.readline()

while line:
    modline = line.replace(‘mispelt’, ‘misspelt’)
    curoff = myfile.tell()
    myfile.seek(curoff - len(line))
    myfile.write(modline)
    print(‘Current position:’, myfile.tell())
    line = myfile.readline()

myfile.close()
```

The function readline() is used prior to the while loop condition (Line 6). To find out that the file-pointer has reached the end-of-file, we need to execute one extra readline(). Thus, if a file contains 10 lines, we need 11 instances of readline(), only the last one returns the empty string. The rest of the code remains the same.

Before reading further, can you spot one issue in this code with respect to the output?

Unfortunately, the output is not as expected.

```
If a word is misspelt it will be corrected.
his is the second line, which also contains misspelt word.
his is the third line.
```

While the two words are corrected, it creates a problem at the start of the lines: T goes missing. Why?

This happens because the new word misspelt is longer than the old one by one character. Therefore, when we write the modified line in Line 10, it overwrites one character of the next line. We show it pictorially below.

| ... | m | i | s | p | e | l | t | | i | t | | w | ... | e | d | . | \n | T | h | i |
|---|---|---|---|---|---|---|---|---|---|---|---|---|---|---|---|---|---|---|---|---|

This buffer gets modified to:

| ... | m | i | s | s | p | e | l | t | | i | t | | w | ... | e | d | . | \n | h | i |
|---|---|---|---|---|---|---|---|---|---|---|---|---|---|---|---|---|---|---|---|---|

A similar issue occurs on the next line too. Thus, unlike our usual variables (such as strings and sequences), we cannot insert text in between a file. We will have to overwrite. In other words, the above program works only when the old and the modified text are of the same length. What happens when the new text is shorter than the original one? You can again use the pictorial buffer representation above to find out the answer.

Can we not fix this problem? We can. Instead of reading line-by-line, if we can read the whole file together, then we can replace all the occurrences of the word and write all the modified contents at once. This is done using a read() function.

```
1. import sys
2.
3. myfile = open(sys.argv[1], 'r+')
4. alllines = myfile.read()
5. modlines = alllines.replace('mispelt', 'misspelt')
6. myfile.seek(0)          # go to the start of the file
7. myfile.write(modlines)
8. myfile.close()
```

Line 4 reads the whole file into alllines variable, on which, we perform find-and-replace (Line 5). We move the file pointer to the start of the file in Line 6, and write the modified lines in Line 7.

You may have an alternative idea that instead of seek() in Line 6, can we not close the file, open it in 'w' mode, and write the modified contents? Yes, that is also feasible.

Another alternative is to use a different output file. Thus, we read lines in a loop from the source file, and write modified lines to the destination file. In such a case, we will always be extending the end-of-file (this is also called as appending to the file) and are not required to seek. The destination file can then be copied to the original source file (our cp.py can be useful).

## File opening modes

Python supports several modes in which files could be opened. We list those below.

| Mode | Meaning | If the file doesn't exist? | If the file exists? |
|---|---|---|---|
| r | Read-only (default) | Returns error | Normal operation |
| w | Write-only | A new one is created | It is truncated to empty file first |
| r+ | Read-Write | Returns error | Normal operation |
| w+ | Read-Write | A new one is created | It is truncated to empty file first |
| a | Append | A new one is created | Writing starts at the end of file |
| x | Write Exclusive | A new one is created | Error |

In addition, it can be specified if the file data would be text or in binary form. In the text form, a number 100 will be written as three bytes (1, 0, 0) whereas in binary, the number can be stored as an integer having four bytes with the appropriate bit pattern (0x00000064). This mode can be combined with any of the primary modes above. A couple of examples are shown below.

| Mode | Meaning | If the file doesn't exist? | If the file exists? |
|---|---|---|---|
| rb | Read-Binary | Returns error | Normal operation |
| wt+ | Read-Write-Text | A new one is created | It is truncated to empty file first |

**Past Connect:** We can store our academic record in a file.

**Example:** Retrieve academic record from a file and compute CGPA.

Recall our academics module in which we kept track of our courses, total points, and earned credits. Our program had hardcoded this academic record. Ideally, this data (academic record) should be kept separate from the functionality (our Python program). We can store this data into a file (*academics.txt*), with semesters separated by an empty line.

```
CS1100 9 10
CS1200 12 9
AM1100 9 9                  # empty line to indicate end of semester
CS2200 12 10
CS2310 6 10
CS2710 6 9                  # this empty line is required
```

Interestingly, our *academics.py* module can remain the same. We can simply modify *academicsuser.py* to read this data file, populate lists in the academics module, and invoke the CGPA calculation. Thus, a sample run would be as follows.

```
$ python3 academicsuser.py academics.txt
course credits earned
CS1100 9 10
CS1200 12 9
AM1100 9 9
This Sem CGPA: 9.3
course credits earned
CS1100 9 10
CS1200 12 9
AM1100 9 9
CS2200 12 10
CS2310 6 10
CS2710 6 9
This Sem CGPA: 9.5
```

Can you write the academicsuser.py program? We present and discuss it below.

```
1.  import sys
2.  from academics import *
3.
4.  acadfile = open(sys.argv[1])
5.
6.  for line in acadfile:
7.      if line == '\n':            # end of semester
8.          cprint()
9.          print("This Sem CGPA:", cgpa(), "\n")
10.     else:
11.         cc, cr, ea = line.split()
12.         add(cc, int(cr), int(ea))
13.
14. acadfile.close()
```

We first import sys for argv, and then all the functions from our module academics (Lines 1 and 2). We open the file specified on the command-line in Line 4. We process each line in the file in the loop at Line 6. If the line is empty, it indicates the end of a semester. So, we print the academic record and CGPA (if block). Otherwise, we split the line into course number, credits, and earned points and add those to our internal record (else block), to be used for CGPA calculation later. We finally close the file in Line 14.

**Example:** Track friends information.

We would like to use files to keep track of friends. A friend is associated with a name and the associated information. We will keep track of the phone number and the github handle. The friends module can provide API to support the following:

| Function | Remarks |
|---|---|
| add(name, phone, github) | Add a new friend |
| remove(name, phone, github) | Remove a friend |
| updatePhone(name, phone) | Update phone number of a friend |
| updateGithub(name, github) | Update github handle of a friend |
| printByName(name) | Print information of a friend |
| printAll() | Print information of all the friends |
| readAll() | Read information of friends from a datafile |
| writeAll() | Write information of friends to the datafile |

We can then call these API functions as follows.

```
1.  add("Somesh", "9934242312", "ssomesh")
2.  add("Shouvick", "+91-8342998727", "shouvickmondal")
3.  add("Jyothi Krishna", "22574374", "jk")
4.  printAll()
5.  writeAll()
6.
7.  readAll()
8.  remove("Somesh")
9.  writeAll()
10.
11. readAll()
12. printAll()
```

We expect the output of this program to be:

```
Somesh 9934242312 ssomesh
Shouvick +91-8342998727 shouvickmondal
Jyothi Krishna 22574374 jk
Shouvick +91-8342998727 shouvickmondal
Jyothi Krishna 22574374 jk
```

where the first three lines are printed due to printAll() of Line 4, while the last two lines due to the same function in Line 12. If we print the contents of the datafile at the end of this processing, those should look as below:

```
Shouvick    +91-8342998727    shouvickmondal
Jyothi Krishna    22574374    jk
```

Can you now implement these API?

Let's first decide how to store the information. As noted by the API, a friend's name is used as a key. Hence, we can store the information using two dictionaries: phones and githubs. The updates to the friends' information happens in these dictionaries. When the user is done with the updates, all the current data can be dumped into a datafile using writeAll(). Before a readAll(), we need to ensure that the dictionaries are empty.

Thus, our friends' module can be written as follows.

```
phones = {}                    # name is the key
githubs = {}                   # name is the key
datafile = “friends.txt”

def add(name, phone, github):
    phones[name] = phone
    githubs[name] = github

def remove(name):
    del(phones[name])
    del(githubs[name])

def updatePhone(name, phone):
    phones[name] = phone

def updateGithub(name, github):
    githubs[name] = github

def get(name):
    return [name, phones[name], githubs[name]]   # list

def printOne(name, phone, github):
    print(name, phone, github)

def printOneList(npg):
    printOne(*npg)

def printByName(name):
    printOneList(get(name))

def printAll():
    for name in phones:
```

```
33.         printByName(name)
34.
35. def writeAll():
36.     global datafile
37.
38. df = open(datafile, ‘w’)
39. for name in phones:
40.     print(name, phones[name], githubs[name], file=df, sep=’\t’)
41. df.close()
42.
43. def readAll():
44.     phones = {}
45.     githubs = {}
46.
47. global datafile
48. df = open(datafile)
49. line = df.readline()
50.
51. while not line == ‘’:
52.     name, phone, github = line.strip().split(‘\t’)
53.     add(name, phone, github)
54.     line = df.readline()
55.
56. df.close()
```

Most of the functions are small and straightforward, accessing the two dictionaries. Let's focus on writeAll() and readAll() functions, which deal with file handling. We use a datafile globally defined (Line 36). This file is opened for writing (Line 37). For each friend's information, we print it in a tab-separated manner into this file in Line 40 (we avoid space-separated values since the name may contain spaces). The function readAll() begins with emptying phones and githubs dictionaries (Lines 44 and 45). The loop at Line 51 goes through all the lines in the datafile. We use strip() to remove newline, and split on tab, to separate the three entities (Line 52), which are then added to the dictionaries (Line 53).

## 4.2 TEXT PROCESSING

Python is well-suited for processing text data, among other aspects. First, string is a basic type supported. Second, there are several functions provided for filtering and manipulating strings. We will explore many of these functions via developing an application's backend.

**Example:** Process conference registration data.

Consider that you have developed a web-form (say, using Google Forms) which collects information of registrants and stores it in a spreadsheet. The basic information supplied is name, email, phone, affiliation, and designation, and the form also captures the time of registration.

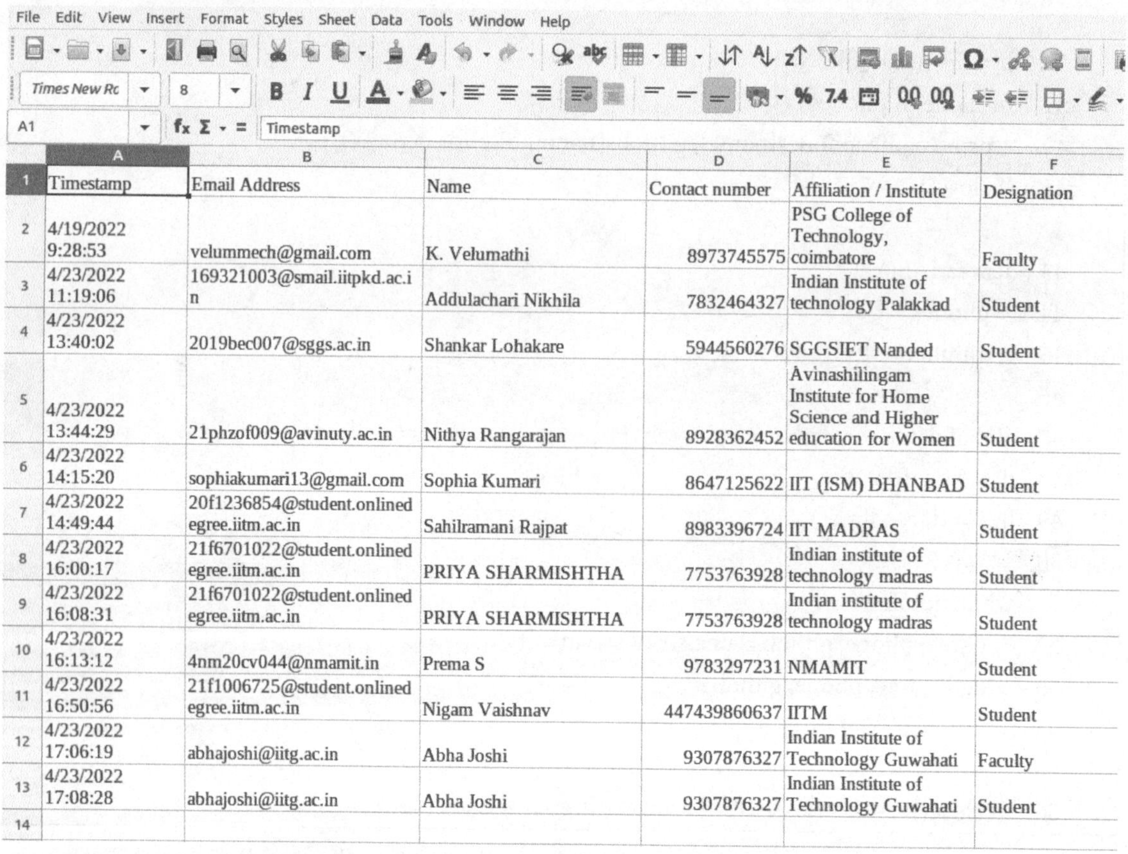


| | A | B | C | D | E | F |
|---|---|---|---|---|---|---|
| 1 | Timestamp | Email Address | Name | Contact number | Affiliation / Institute | Designation |
| 2 | 4/19/2022 9:28:53 | velummech@gmail.com | K. Velumathi | 8973745575 | PSG College of Technology, coimbatore | Faculty |
| 3 | 4/23/2022 11:19:06 | 169321003@smail.iitpkd.ac.in | Addulachari Nikhila | 7832464327 | Indian Institute of technology Palakkad | Student |
| 4 | 4/23/2022 13:40:02 | 2019bec007@sggs.ac.in | Shankar Lohakare | 5944560276 | SGGSIET Nanded | Student |
| 5 | 4/23/2022 13:44:29 | 21phzof009@avinuty.ac.in | Nithya Rangarajan | 8928362452 | Avinashilingam Institute for Home Science and Higher education for Women | Student |
| 6 | 4/23/2022 14:15:20 | sophiakumari13@gmail.com | Sophia Kumari | 8647125622 | IIT (ISM) DHANBAD | Student |
| 7 | 4/23/2022 14:49:44 | 20f1236854@student.onlinedegree.iitm.ac.in | Sahilramani Rajpat | 8983396724 | IIT MADRAS | Student |
| 8 | 4/23/2022 16:00:17 | 21f6701022@student.onlinedegree.iitm.ac.in | PRIYA SHARMISHTHA | 7753763928 | Indian institute of technology madras | Student |
| 9 | 4/23/2022 16:08:31 | 21f6701022@student.onlinedegree.iitm.ac.in | PRIYA SHARMISHTHA | 7753763928 | Indian institute of technology madras | Student |
| 10 | 4/23/2022 16:13:12 | 4nm20cv044@nmamit.in | Prema S | 9783297231 | NMAMIT | Student |
| 11 | 4/23/2022 16:50:56 | 21f1006725@student.onlinedegree.iitm.ac.in | Nigam Vaishnav | 447439860637 | IITM | Student |
| 12 | 4/23/2022 17:06:19 | abhajoshi@iitg.ac.in | Abha Joshi | 9307876327 | Indian Institute of Technology Guwahati | Faculty |
| 13 | 4/23/2022 17:08:28 | abhajoshi@iitg.ac.in | Abha Joshi | 9307876327 | Indian Institute of Technology Guwahati | Student |
| 14 | | | | | | |

There are libraries which support processing of spreadsheets. In our application, we can convert it into a text-based .csv (comma-separated values) file, so that it can be processed as a tabular data.

Timestamp, Email Address, Name, Contact number, Affiliation / Institute, Designation

4/19/2022 9:28:53, velummech@gmail.com, K. Velumathi, 8973745575, PSG College of Technology, coimbatore, Faculty

4/23/2022 11:19:06, 169321003@smail.iitpkd.ac.in, Addulachari Nikhila, 7832464327, Indian Institute of technology Palakkad, Student

4/23/2022 13:40:02,2019bec007@sggs.ac.in, Shankar Lohakare, 5944560276, SGGSIET Nanded, Student

4/23/2022 13:44:29, 21phzof009@avinuty.ac.in, Nithya Rangarajan, 8928362452, Avinashilingam Institute for Home Science and Higher education for Women , Student

4/23/2022 14:15:20, sophiakumari13@gmail.com, Sophia Kumari, 8647125622, IIT (ISM) DHANBAD, Student

4/23/2022 14:49:44, 20f1236854@student.onlinedegree.iitm.ac.in, Sahilramani Rajpat, 8983396724, IIT MADRAS, Student

4/23/2022 16:00:17, 21f6701022@student.onlinedegree.iitm.ac.in, PRIYA SHARMISHTHA, 7753763928, Indian institute of technology madras ,Student

4/23/2022 16:08:31, 21f6701022@student.onlinedegree.iitm.ac.in, PRIYA SHARMISHTHA, 7753763928, Indian institute of technology madras ,Student

4/23/2022 16:13:12,4nm20cv044@nmamit.in,Prema S,9783297231,NMAMIT,Student

4/23/2022 16:50:56, 21f1006725@student.onlinedegree.iitm.ac.in, Nigam Vaishnav, 447439860637, IITM, Student

4/23/2022 17:06:19, abhajoshi@iitg.ac.in, Abha Joshi, 9307876327, Indian Institute of Technology Guwahati, Faculty

4/23/2022 17:08:28, abhajoshi@iitg.ac.in, Abha Joshi, 9307876327, Indian Institute of Technology Guwahati, Student

**Challenge 1:** Comma is present in the data.

While other fields are okay, the affiliation field may contain a comma. Even while typing a name, someone may inadvertently enter a comma instead of a dot (e.g. P. V, Sindhu). Someone may enter two phone numbers separated by a comma. All of these are real-world problems. One way to ensure valid data is by having validation checks at the form-level itself, which can handle these problems, ensuring that when the data reaches your Python script, it is *sanitized*. Another way is to not assume that the data is sanitized, but write our script to handle these situations.

**Solution:** We can solve this comma problem by saving the spreadsheet in .csv format with tab (\t) as the separator. Typically (but not always), a tab is not present in the form-input data. Another option is to encode the data using the *base64* module, which allows arbitrary binary data also to be processed. In our program, we will use tab-separated values.

**Challenge 2:** Some fields may contain a newline.

By default, our script may assume that one registration record appears in one line of the .csv file. However, a few fields such as address may contain a newline, which may result in the malfunctioning of our script. Often entering a newline is not directly feasible in usual text-boxes on forms, but when the data is copy-pasted from elsewhere, newlines may appear. Textarea boxes in HTML can also have newline characters.

1. 4/19/2022 9:28:53, velummech@gmail.com, K. Velumathi, 8973745575, “PSG College of Technology
2. coimbatore”, Faculty
3. 4/23/2022 11:19:06, 169321003@smail.iitpkd.ac.in, Addulachari Nikhila, 7832464327, “Indian Institute of technology
4. Palakkad” Student

**Solution:** Similar to handling commas, the validation logic (typically, in JavaScript for HTML forms) can either disallow newlines, or convert those to a different form (such as <br> in HTML). Alternatively, while converting from spreadsheet to CSV format, double-quotes can be used as the text-delimiter, which stores multiline field in double-quotes (if double-quotes are present in the field, those can be encoded, or escaped as \" or “”). In our program, we will assume that this is taken care of in a preprocessing step, and each line is a new record.

**Challenge 3:** Header can be mistakenly recognized as a record.

Our .csv file contains the first line as the header. While processing, if we forget, our functions may treat it as a valid record, which can change the output. For instance, if we are booking rooms for all the attendees, we may end up booking (and paying for) one more room than required.

**Solution:** This is easy to resolve. We can simply remove it as a sanitization prepass. Alternatively, our Python script can skip the first line.

With these challenges and possible solutions, let's now find out some interesting statistics from the registration data. How do we represent the data? We can store each column as a list. Thus, for our example data, we can have six associative lists for timestamps, emails, names, phones, affiliations, and designations. These are populated by reading the .csv file.

**Functionality 1:** Find the number of non-students registered.

This is a simple check on designation (populated from a drop-down menu in the registration form).

```
def nonStudents():
    for ii in range(len(designations)):
        if not designations[ii] == 'Student':
            printRecord(ii)
```

We make use of the auxiliary function printRecord() to print details of a registrant. The final output of using the above function is:

```
K. Velumathi:::PSG College of Technology, coimbatore:::Faculty:::velummech@gmail.
com:::8973745575
Abha Joshi:::Indian Institute of Technology Guwahati:::Faculty:::abhajoshi@iitg.ac.in:::9307876327
```

**Functionality 2:** Find all the people registered from IITs.

This is again a straightforward check on the affiliation, with the caveat that some people may use IIT or iit or Indian Institute of Technology or INDIAN INSTITUTE OF TECHNOLOGY.

```
def iit():
    for ii in range(len(affiliations)):
        lowaffil = affiliations[ii].lower()      # to lower-case

        if ("iit" in lowaffil and not "iiit" in lowaffil) or \
            "indian institute of technology" in lowaffil:
            printRecord(ii)
```

Line 7 uses a string function lower() to convert the affiliation to lower-case. This allows us to avoid any capitalization issues while comparing strings. We check if it is "iit" or its full-form in the condition on Lines 9 and 10. Since we know that there would be registrants from IIIT also, we filter those out from the output. The final output of using the above function is:

```
Addulachari Nikhila:::Indian Institute of technology Palakkad:::Student:::169321003@smail.iitpkd.
ac.in:::7832464327
Sophia Kumari:::IIT (ISM) DHANBAD :::Student:::sophiakumari13@gmail.com:::8647125622
PRIYA SHARMISHTHA:::Indian institute of technology madras :::Student:::21f6701022@student.
onlinedegree.iitm.ac.in:::7753763928
Priya Sharmishtha:::Indian institute of technology madras :::Student:::21f6701022@student.
onlinedegree.iitm.ac.in:::7753763928
Nigam Vaishnav:::IITM:::Student:::21f1006725@student.onlinedegree.iitm.ac.in:::447439860637
Abha Joshi:::Indian Institute of Technology Guwahati:::Faculty:::abhajoshi@iitg.ac.in:::9307876327
Abha Joshi:::Indian Institute of Technology Guwahati:::Student:::abhajoshi@iitg.ac.in:::9307876327
```

**Functionality 3:** Find all the duplicate records.

Finding duplicates can be done by checking all pairs of records. We can also reduce the number of checks between a pair to decide them to be duplicates. For instance, in our code, we will say two records match if the names and the email ids match (even if the remaining information is different). You can have more stringent checks by adding more conditions.

```
12. def match(ii, jj):
13.     return (names[ii].upper() == names[jj].upper() and \
14.             emails[ii].upper() == emails[jj].upper())
15.
16. def duplicates():
17.     for ii in range(len(timestamps)):
18.         for jj in range(ii + 1, len(timestamps)):
19.             if match(ii, jj):
20.                 print("Records", ii, "and", jj, "are duplicates")
21.                 printRecord(ii)
22.                 printRecord(jj)
```

Enumerating all pairs can be done using a nested loop (Lines 17 and 18). If the two records match (Line 19), then we print them. The match() function uses the string function upper() to remove any differences in the capitalization. Output of using the above function is:

```
Records 6 and 8 are duplicates
PRIYA SHARMISHTHA:::Indian institute of technology madras :::Student:::21f6701022@student.
onlinedegree.iitm.ac.in:::7753763928
Priya Sharmishtha:::Indian institute of technology madras :::Student:::21f6701022@student.
onlinedegree.iitm.ac.in:::7753763928
Records 10 and 11 are duplicates
Abha Joshi:::Indian Institute of Technology Guwahati:::Faculty:::abhajoshi@iitg.ac.in:::9307876327
Abha Joshi:::Indian Institute of Technology Guwahati:::Student:::abhajoshi@iitg.ac.in:::9307876327
```

**Functionality 4:** Display a list of participants grouped by their affiliations.

Such a grouping can be done in a manner similar to Functionality 3's nested loops. But we can as well sort the lists based on affiliations to have the registrants with the same affiliation in consecutive records. Unfortunately, this poses another challenge. We have multiple associative lists. So if we want to sort the affiliations list, we should accordingly also sort other lists. Python provides a zip() function to achieve this.

```
23. def groupByAffiliation():
24.     grouped = zip(affiliations, names, emails)
25.     sg = sorted(grouped)
26.
27.     for record in sg:
28.         print(record[0], record[1], record[2], sep=":::")
```

Line 24 creates a joint aggregate from individual aggregates. This joint aggregate is sorted in Line 25, which sorts all the associative lists. Note that we have provided *affiliations* as the first list in zip(). Once these lists are sorted based on affiliation, we go over this sorted aggregate row-by-row, that is, one index across all three aggregates (Line 27). Each entry in this row corresponds to one record. Thus, *record[0]* corresponds to the first affiliation in the sorted order, *record[1]* is the name corresponding to it, and *record[2]* is the email id of that registrant. We print this record in Line 28. The output using the above function is:

```
Avinashilingam Institute for Home Science and Higher education for Women :::Nithya Rangarajan:::21phzof009@avinuty.ac.in
IIIT Kancheepuram :::Sahilramani Rajpat:::sahil@student.iiitdm.ac.in
IIT (ISM) DHANBAD :::Sophia Kumari:::sophiakumari13@gmail.com
IITM:::Nigam Vaishnav:::21f1006725@student.onlinedegree.iitm.ac.in
Indian Institute of Technology Guwahati:::Abha Joshi:::abhajoshi@iitg.ac.in
Indian Institute of Technology Guwahati:::Abha Joshi:::abhajoshi@iitg.ac.in
Indian Institute of technology Palakkad:::Addulachari Nikhila:::169321003@smail.iitpkd.ac.in
Indian institute of technology madras :::PRIYA SHARMISHTHA:::21f6701022@student.onlinedegree.iitm.ac.in
Indian institute of technology madras :::Priya Sharmishtha:::21f6701022@student.onlinedegree.iitm.ac.in
NMAMIT:::Prema S:::4nm20cv044@nmamit.in
PSG College of Technology, coimbatore:::K. Velumathi:::velummech@gmail.com
SGGSIET Nanded :::Shankar Lohakare :::2019bec007@sggs.ac.in
```

The whole code, being large, is made available on the book's code page[1]. We discussed the most important parts of it here.

1 http://www.cse.iitm.ac.in/~rupesh/books/python/code/unit4/

## Useful string methods

Following is a glimpse of various useful string methods supported.

Assume that s = “beauty brought butter, butter was bitter, so she brought more butter to make bitter butter better.”

| Function | Meaning | Usage | Output |
|---|---|---|---|
| string * number | Repeat a string | for i in range(5):<br>    print(‘*’ * i) | *<br>**<br>***<br>**** |
| count(substr) | Number of occurrences of a substring | s.count(‘ter’) | 7 |
| find(substr) | First index of substring | s.find(‘ter’)<br>s.find(‘terse’) | 18<br>–1 |
| [start:end] | Substring or slicing | s[18:22]<br>s[:5]<br>s[–5:-2]<br>s[5::–1] | ter,<br>beaut<br>tte<br>ytuaeb |
| startswith(substr)<br>endswith(substr) | If a string starts or ends with a substring | s.startswith(‘bea’)<br>s.endswith(‘ter’) | True<br>False |
| replace(oldsubstr, newsubstr) | Replace all occurrences of a substring by another | s.replace(“butter”, “butter and batter”) | # find it out |
| title()<br>upper()<br>lower()<br>swapcase()<br>istitle()<br><br>isupper()<br>islower() | First letter of each word capital and all others lowercase<br>All uppercase<br>All lowercase<br>Alter case<br>First letter of each word capital and all others lowercase?<br>All uppercase?<br>All lowercase? | “I aM iN.”.title()<br>“I am in.”.upper()<br>“I am In.”.lower()<br>“I am In.”.swapcase()<br><br>“I Am IN”.istitle()<br>“I AM IN”.isupper()<br>“i am in”.islower() | I Am In.<br>I AM IN.<br>i am in.<br>i AM iN.<br>False<br>True<br>True |
| isalpha()<br><br>isalnum()<br><br>isdigit()<br><br>isspace() | All characters are [a-zA-Z]?<br><br>All characters are [a-zA-Z0-9]?<br><br>All characters are [0-9]?<br><br>All characters are whitespaces. | “IaMIn”.isalpha()<br>“I AM IN”.isalpha()<br>“rupesh0508”.isalnum()<br>“0.5”.isalnum()<br>“9940288482”.isdigit()<br>“99402 88482”.isdigit()<br>“ \t \n”.isspace()<br>“ \t \n\\”.isspace() | True<br>False<br>True<br>False<br>True<br>False<br>True<br>False |
| join() | Separate each element of a list by a substring. In this case, each element is a character. | “#”.join(“I am in.”)<br>“.”.join([“iitm”, “ac”, “in”]) | I# #a#m# #i#n#.<br>iitm.ac.in |
| zfill(width) | Lead string by zeros to fill-up width. | “483”.zfill(10)<br>“–483”.zfill(10)<br>“Hello”.zfill(10) | 0000000483<br>–000000483<br>00000Hello |

## 4.3 PATTERN MATCHING AND REGULAR EXPRESSIONS

Sometimes, an exact match cannot be specified to cover all the cases. Consider, for instance, finding a mobile number from a text. One may find it easy to go over the text and identify ten consecutive digits. This is alright, but sometimes the mobile number is written in different forms, such as 99406 67821 (with a space or a hyphen), while at times as (994) 066-7821 (e.g., in the US). One can write a program to identify all such patterns. Regular expressions allow us to specify those patterns succinctly.

Python provides a module re for regular expressions. We will start with a function findall() to identify all occurrences of a given pattern in a text.

**Example:** Find all the mobile numbers out of a long text.

We will first show the program and then explain.

```
1.  import re
2.
3.  text = “””
4.  Hello, I am Dr. Mobile123. Please call me in case of an emergency. My phone number is 99405
    33241. Otherwise, you can call my assistant at 8932732436. I am available at my clinic from 9 to
    1. For appointments, call the reception at (687) 324-3232.
5.  “””
6.
7.  digits10 = r’\d{10}’                              # 10 consecutive digits
8.  digits55 = r’\d{5}\D\d{5}’                         # 5 digits gap 5 digits
9.  digitsus = r’\(\d{3}\)\s?\d{3}\D\d{4}’             # (3 digits) 3 digits - 4 digits
10.
11. regex = digits10 + ‘|’ + digits55 + ‘|’ + digitsus  # first or second or third pattern
12. mobiles = re.findall(regex, text)
13. print(mobiles)
```

The output of the above program is:

```
['99405 33241', '8932732436', '(687) 324-3232']
```

One can, of course, go over this mobile list to print an individual mobile number identified from the text.

Let's understand the code carefully. Line 3 creates a long piece of text (in triple-quotes). It contains numbers multiple times, but contains mobile numbers only thrice in different formats. The first format is listed as a raw string in Line 7. \d indicates a digit and \d{10} indicates ten digits. This is a regular expression (as understood by the re module). It matches 8932732436, but not the other two. The second pattern in Line 8 matches 99405 33241 and does not match the other two. It looks for five digits \d{5}, then a non-digit \D (such as space or hyphen), followed by another set of five digits. The third pattern on Line 9 for US mobile format consists of an opening parenthesis \( followed by three digits \d{3} followed by a closing parenthesis, followed by an optional space \s?, followed by three digits \d{3}, followed by a non-digit \D (such as space or hyphen), followed finally by four digits \d{4}. \s indicates a whitespace character, ? makes the preceding expression optional, and parenthesis need to be escaped because those have a special meaning in re.

These three patterns are OR'ed in the regular expression regex at Line 11 using | operator (understood by the re module). Line 12 then calls the findall() method which finds all occurrences of the regular expression in text. These are returned as a list.

Is it possible to have a single regular expression for 99405 33241 and 8932732436? Yes, we can modify digits55 as '\d{5}\D?\d{5}' and it will match both the phone numbers.

**Good Programming Practice:** It is easy to make the regular expressions complex. Therefore, split those into multiple parts, test each of them separately, and then join them, as we have done in the above example.

**Example:** Find all email addresses out of a long text.

Before reading further, think about how you want to identify an email address. One possibility is to have alphanumeric characters, followed by symbol @, followed by another set of alphanumeric characters. An alphanumeric character (including underscore) can be specified as \w. Thus, our regular expression should be: (one or more \w)@(one or more \w).

```
1. import re
2.
3. text = "My departmental email id is rupesh@cse.iitm.ac.in. This is what I use for all the official purposes. The institute also provides an id rupesh@iitm.ac.in. During PhD, I used to have a personal email id rupesh0something@gmail.com, which is still in use. When gmail was not around, id rupesh_something@usa.net was the one I used. I also own a twitter handle @ rupeshsomething, which I hardly use. That's it from my side for now. See you in class @11."
4.
5. regex = r'\w+@\w+'
6. emails = re.findall(regex, text.lower())          # use lower-case string
7. print(emails)
```

Symbol + in the regular expression on Line 5 indicates one or more occurrences of the preceding expression. We also encourage you to use lower() or upper() functions (as in Line 6) where applicable, so the regular expressions need to take care of only one case.

What will be the output of the above program?

```
['rupesh@cse', 'rupesh@iitm', 'rupesh0something@gmail', 'rupeshsomething@usa']
```

One good aspect of this output is that the twitter handle and the class timing strings are not included. But although the output is close to what we want, it is not accurate. This happened because \w does not include a dot, which is present in the domain-name of the email address. Let's include that then by changing Line 5 to:

```
5. regex = r'\w+@[\w\.]+'
```

The subexpression prior to @ remains the same. The one after that groups \w and . together using [...] and adds + to it for one or more. Can you guess the output with this modified regular expression?

If you felt the output was correct, that is not fully true. Here it is, including the full-stop at the end of email addresses (since we have now included a dot).

```
['rupesh@cse.iitm.ac.in.', 'rupesh@iitm.ac.in.', 'rupesh0something@gmail.com', 'rupesh_something@usa.net']
```

How do we handle this? We want dot to be present in the domain-name, but it should not be the last character of the domain. We can specify that by modifying the regular expression as:

5. regex = r'\w+@[\w\.]+\w'

We simply added another \w at the end, which permits all the characters except the dot in the end. Now the output is as expected.

```
['rupesh@cse.iitm.ac.in', 'rupesh@iitm.ac.in', 'rupesh0something@gmail.com', 'rupesh_something@usa.net']
```

**Discussion:** While we learned multiple aspects about specifying a regular expression, the regular expression above is not the most precise one. For instance, an email id rupesh@iitm........a is matched by this regular expression, which is not a valid one. We will have to modify it to include at least one \w between dots.

Following are the various operators supported by the regular expressions.

<table>
<tr><th>Expression</th><th>Matches</th><th>Example</th><th>Outcome</th></tr>
<tr><td>hello</td><td>substring hello</td><td>mispelt</td><td>Finds all occurrences of mispelt.</td></tr>
<tr><td>\d</td><td>one digit</td><td>\d\d</td><td>Two digit number such as minutes</td></tr>
<tr><td>\w</td><td>letter, number, underscore</td><td>\w\w\w\w</td><td>Four letters such as I18N</td></tr>
<tr><td>\s</td><td>whitespace</td><td>hello\sworld</td><td>hello world</td></tr>
<tr><td>a+</td><td>one or more occurrences of a</td><td>ab+</td><td>Matches ab, abb, abbb, abbbb, ...</td></tr>
<tr><td>a*</td><td>zero or more occurrences of a</td><td>ab*c</td><td>Matches ac, abc, abbc, abbbc, ...</td></tr>
<tr><td>a?</td><td>zero or one occurrence of a</td><td>ab?c</td><td>Matches only ac and abc</td></tr>
<tr><td>.</td><td>any character except \n</td><td>a.c</td><td>Matches abc, aac, acc, a-c, a+c, a c, ...</td></tr>
<tr><td>[abc]</td><td>either a or b or c (single char)</td><td>[+b2]</td><td>Matches + or b or 2</td></tr>
<tr><td>a|b</td><td>either a or b (as patterns)</td><td>Hi|Hello</td><td>Matches Hi or Hello</td></tr>
<tr><td>a{3}</td><td>matches aaa</td><td>O{3}H</td><td>Matches OOOH</td></tr>
<tr><td>a{3, 5}</td><td>matches aaa, aaaa, aaaaa</td><td>O{3, 5}H</td><td>Matches OOOH, OOOOH, OOOOOH</td></tr>
</table>

Below are a few commonly occurring patterns.

| Requirement | Regular expression |
|---|---|
| Variable names | [a–zA–Z_][a–zA–Z_0-9]* |
| Pincode | \d{6} or [1-9]\d{5} |
| Aadhar number | \d{12} or \d{4}\s\d{4}\s\d{4} or \d{4}\D\d{4}\D\d{4} |

<table>
<tr><th>Requirement</th><th>Regular expression</th></tr>
<tr><td>PAN</td><td>[A–Z]{5}\d{4}[A–Z]</td></tr>
<tr><td>Social Security Number (US)</td><td>\d{3}–\d{2}–\d{4}</td></tr>
<tr><td>Real number</td><td>[0–9]+\.[0–9]+</td></tr>
<tr><td>Website</td><td>(http://)?X(\.X)+ where X is [a–zA–Z_0-9–]+</td></tr>
<tr><td>IP address</td><td>\d+(\.\d+){3}</td></tr>
<tr><td>Date in dd/mm/yy format</td><td>\d\d/\d\d/\d\d</td></tr>
<tr><td>A student roll number such as CS22B018</td><td>[A–Z][A–Z]\d\d[A–Z]\d\d\d</td></tr>
<tr><td>Weight of an item</td><td>\d+\s*(kg|lb|gm)</td></tr>
<tr><td>Movie names of the Golmaal series</td><td>Golmaal((\s|–)(2|3|Again))?</td></tr>
</table>

**Example:** Find dates from a text.

You must have come across a feature in gmail which automatically finds the mention of dates in an email, clicking which allows you to add an event in your calendar on that date. While we will not solve this larger problem, we will solve a part of it. In particular, we will allow dates of the following forms to be identified.

September 10, 2023

Sept. 10, 2023

Sep. 10, 2023

Aug 5, 2023

Jan 5

Feb 5 23

Can you write a regular expression to recognize the above patterns?

Here is the text.

```
text = “””
Hello Prashant
How is Bangalore treating you? Do you continue to be in the same company?
I wanted to check if you are around on September 10, 2023? I am coming there for an official visit
on Sep 9 and would like to drop by your house in the evening of sept 10.
If that is not feasible, I may have to come back in October. Are you around on oct 10? or oct. 11?
Do let me know.
“””
```

We want the output of our program to recognize the highlighted dates (and nothing else, such as only October). We build the regular expression using twelve months' names.

```
1.  months = (‘jan’, ‘feb’, ‘mar’, ‘apr’, ‘may’, ‘jun’, ‘jul’, ‘aug’, ‘sep’, ‘oct’, ‘nov’, ‘dec’)
2.  regex12 = ‘’
3.
4.  for mm in months:
5.      regex12 = regex12 + mm + ‘|’     # create regex using 12 months
6.
7.  regex12 = ‘(‘ + regex12[:-1] + ‘)’     # remove the extra |
8.  finalregex = ‘(‘ + regex12 + r’[a-z.]*\s+\d\d?)(,?\s?\d{2,4})?’
9.
10. dates = re.findall(finalregex, text.lower())
11.
12. for onedate in dates:
13.     print(onedate)
```

We explain various parts of the regular expression on Line 8. Variable regex12 contains the three-letter abbreviations of the twelve months separated by |. [a-z.]* allows the month to contain either only the abbreviation, or the full name, or anything in between, including a dot. This needs to be followed by at least one space. \d\d? matches one or two digits of the day. This is optionally followed by the second part of the pattern which may contain comma and space, followed by the year in two, three, or four digits. If you wish to support only two or four digit year, it can be achieved as \d{2}|\d{4}.

The output of the whole program is:

```
('september 10', 'sep', ', 2023')
('sep 9', 'sep', '')
('sept 10', 'sep', '')
('oct 10', 'oct', '')
('oct. 11', 'oct', '')
```

Each tuple in the output contains three entries corresponding to the three parenthesized expressions in our regular expression: month followed by day, month in *regex12*, and optional part of the year.

Discussion: The function *findall()* finds all the occurrences of the given regular expression. If you are interested only in one, you can use the *search()* function. For instance:

```
match = re.search(r’Golmaal((\s|-)(2|3|Again))?’, ‘I watched Golmaal Again again.’)
if match: print(match)
```

## 4.4 APPLICATION: QUERYING PUBLICATION DATA

We put all our learning together to create a real-world application. We are given publication data from Scopus, and we would like to query it to identify various records of interest. Snapshot of the data is given below. Its first line shows various columns such as Authors, Author(s) ID, Title, Year, etc.

| | A | B | C | D | E | F |
|---|---|---|---|---|---|---|
| 1 | Authors | Author(s) ID | Title | Year | Source title | Volume |
| 2 | Sai, A.B., Mohankumar, A.K., Khap | 57204471877;57216695737;5754 | A Survey of Evaluation Metrics Used for NLG Systems | 2023 | ACM Computing Surveys | 5 |
| 3 | Kondaveeti, S., Govindarajan, D., M | 55314053500;57200212304;2273 | Sustainable bioelectrochemical systems for bioenergy generation via waste | 2023 | Fuel | 33 |
| 4 | Boominathan, A., Vijaya, R. | 8853819600;57211074463; | Numerical Modelling of Basin Effects on Earthquake Ground Motions in Kut | 2023 | Springer Tracts in Civil Engineering | |
| 5 | Ishwarya S, P., Dugyala, V.R., Prad | 57426253900;55789982900;5610 | Sessile drop evaporation approach to detect starch adulteration in milk | 2023 | Food Control | 14 |
| 6 | Wani, S., Samala, R., Kandasami, R | 57853087700;57208178391;5580 | Numerical Study on the Effect of Hydrate Saturation on the Geo-Mechanical | 2023 | Lecture Notes in Civil Engineering | 288 LNCE |
| 7 | Gosavi, H.S., Pratapa, P.P., Mallad | 57822141500;37010429300;5580 | Band Gap Estimation of D-LEGO Meta-structures Using FRF-Based Substr | 2023 | Conference Proceedings of the Society for Experimen | |
| 8 | Jain, P., Chavan, T., Chakraborty, M | 57653315500;57458696100;5722 | Computational Study of Aero-acoustic Feedback in Supersonic Cavity Flow | 2023 | Lecture Notes in Mechanical Engineering | |
| 9 | Ramanujachari, V., Roy, R.D., Amru | 7801673060;8596973800;572155 | Design and Performance Evaluation of Plug Nozzle for Rotating Detonation | 2023 | Lecture Notes in Mechanical Engineering | |
| 10 | Revulagadda, A.P., Adapa, B.R., Gd | 57821629200;57820849900;5719 | A Numerical Investigation on the Effect of Lip Geometry with Tangential Film | 2023 | Lecture Notes in Mechanical Engineering | |
| 11 | Chakraborty, A., Das, M., Sahu, S., | 56258611200;56091500300;3650 | A Parametric Study on Rotary Slinger Spray Characteristics Using Laser Dia | 2023 | Lecture Notes in Mechanical Engineering | |
| 12 | Kumawat, S.K., Ghugare, A.D., Kum | 57821112300;56081589500;5720 | Nanoboron Slurry Fuel Droplet Combustion for High-Particle Loading Ratio | 2023 | Lecture Notes in Mechanical Engineering | |
| 13 | Sekar, A., Chakraborty, M., Vaidyan | 57429823900;57221536090;1633 | Numerical Investigation of Blockage of Scramjet Strut Injector Model in a Sc | 2023 | Lecture Notes in Mechanical Engineering | |
| 14 | Ramanujachari, V., Dutta Roy, R., A | 7801673060;57821107300;57215 | Design and Analysis of Rotating Detonation Wave Engine | 2023 | Lecture Notes in Mechanical Engineering | |
| 15 | Udupa K, A., Alagappan, P. | 57811996400;37107303700; | Segmentation Based on Image Analysis of Concrete | 2023 | Structural Integrity | 2 |
| 16 | Mohanty, A.S., Rao, B.N. | 57612136100;57812674600; | Nonlinear Finite Element Analysis of Corroded Prestressed Beams | 2023 | Structural Integrity | 2 |
| 17 | Mourya, U., Jayachandran, A. | 57673849500;57217795173; | Evaluation of Second-Order Effects in Cold-Formed Steel Pallet Racks | 2023 | Structural Integrity | 2 |
| 18 | Raja, N., Balasubramaniam, K. | 57202348188;7005602178; | Remote Excitation Ultrasonic Waveguide-Based SHM for Critical Application | 2023 | Lecture Notes in Civil Engineering | 270 LNCE |
| 19 | Gantasala, S., Thomas, T., Rajagop | 57806950500;57188585660;1513 | Spherical Inclusions Based Defect Modes in a Phononic Crystal for Piezoel | 2023 | Lecture Notes in Civil Engineering | 270 LNCE |
| 20 | Sharma, B.N., Kapuria, S., Arockiar | 57211516528;7004458697;16480 | Damage Detection Using Refined Time Reversal Method of Lamb Waves Ur | 2023 | Lecture Notes in Civil Engineering | 254 LNCE |
| 21 | Dixit, S., Kumar, D., Dash, B.B., Su | 57878213200;57671391100;5787 | Effect of solutionizing temperature and cooling rate on phase morphology, re | 2022 | Journal of Alloys and Compounds | 92 |
| 22 | Karati, A., Ghosh, S., Nagini, M., M | 57194570176;57200726297;5544 | Thermoelectric properties of nanocrystalline half-Heusler high-entropy Ti2Ni | 2022 | Journal of Alloys and Compounds | 92 |
| 23 | Kale, A.V., Krishnasamy, A. | 57438773300;57202644792; | Experimental investigation on operating light-duty diesel engine using etha | 2022 | Fuel | 33 |

By now, we know how to convert this data into a .csv file and read the records in various lists. Note that all the authors are part of the same column. Since author names can be ambiguous or written differently in different documents (e.g., R. Nasre or Rupesh Nasre), Scopus maintains a unique ID per author, which is given in the second column. We would like to query this information. All the code along with sample data is available on the course webpage[2]. We note that there is a difference in the way Windows and Linux store newline characters in files. Therefore, your program may not directly work across the platforms. To ease out your processing, the course webpage lists files in both 'dos' (for Windows) and 'unix' (for Linux) formats. Also, to handle special characters in Windows, one may need to change the encoding to UTF 8 as follows.

df = open(datafile, **encoding**='utf8')

**Functionality 1:** Print all the documents of an author, with the author's name.

For instance, for query string 'Nasre Rupesh', the output would be:

```
"Pattipati, D.K., Nasre, R., Puligundla, S.K.":::56593174200;35275730500;57204369664;":::BOLD: an ontology-based log debugger for C programs",2022
"Singh, S., Shah, T., Nasre, R.":::57202881568;57468012500;35275730500;":::ParTBC: Faster Estimation of Top-k Betweenness Centrality Vertices on GPU",2022
"Muniasamy, R.P., Nasre, R., Narayanaswamy, N.S.":::57355590000;35275730500;8935093600;":::Accelerating Computation of Steiner Trees on GPUs",2022
```

We list only a few columns, separated by :::. Note that the record does not mention the author name as 'Nasre Rupesh', but as 'Nasre, R.' as a substring. We achieve this by generating name variants using the following functions. Thus, for 'Nasre Rupesh', the variants are 'Nasre Rupesh', 'Nasre\W*R\W*' and 'N\W*Rupesh\W*'.

```
def getNameVariant(words, nn):
    ii = 0
    namevv = '';

    for ww in words:
```

2 http://www.cse.iitm.ac.in/~rupesh/books/python/code/unit4/

```
        if ii == nn:
            namevv = namevv + ww + ‘W*’
        elif not ww == ‘’:
            namevv = namevv + ww[0] + ‘W*’

        ii = ii + 1

    return namevv.strip()

def getNameVariants(author):
    variants = [author]
    words = author.split(‘ ’)

    for ii in range(len(words)):
        # ii’th word needs to be left as it is, others need to be shortened.
        vv = getNameVariant(words, ii)
        variants.append(vv)

    return variants
```

The outer function getNameVariants() splits an author name into words, and calls getNameVariant() function to shorten all but one word.

**Functionality 2:** Print all the documents of an author, with the author’s ID.

Implementing this functionality is relatively easy, since author IDs can be checked for an exact match. Its output is the same as Functionality 1 for ‘35275730500’, but can be different (fewer records) due to exact match. For instance, for input ‘Vignesh’ Functionality 1 outputs several records corresponding to multiple Vigneshs, while with input ‘57195129630’, there is a single record.

```
def allOfAuthorById(aid):
    for ii in range(len(authornames)):
        if aid in authorids[ii]:
            printRecord(ii)
```

The function goes over all the records and wherever it finds the given author-id, that record is printed.

**Functionality 3:** Print all the documents of a first author.

For instance, for input ‘Muniasamy Rajesh’, the output is:

```
"Muniasamy, R.P., Nasre, R., Narayanaswamy, N.S.":::57355590000;35275730500;8935093600;":::Acce
lerating Computation of Steiner Trees on GPUs",2022
```

This functionality needs peeping into author-names and querying only the first one. One possibility is to extract all the author names into a list and then checking only the first elements. This would be useful in the next functionality also. We will do it in a slightly different way using regular expressions. We observe that the first author is characterized by a double-quote. We exploit this to check the first author.

```
1.    match = re.search(r’”[^,”]*’ + author.upper(), authornames[ii].upper())
2.    if match: printRecord(ii)
```

The regular expression in Line 1 looks for a double-quote character followed by non-comma non-double-quote characters (signifying the first author).

**Functionality 4:** Print all the documents of a non-first author.

This is a flip of the previous functionality, and we implement it using Functionality 1 and 3 – that, find a document with an author, and then check whether it is the first author. If not, we output it.

For instance, for input ‘Nasre Rupesh’, the output is:

```
"Pattipati, D.K., Nasre, R., Puligundla, S.K.":::56593174200;35275730500;57204369664;":::BOLD: an ontology-based log debugger for C programs",2022
"Singh, S., Shah, T., Nasre, R.":::57202881568;57468012500;35275730500;":::ParTBC: Faster Estimation of Top-k Betweenness Centrality Vertices on GPU",2022
"Muniasamy, R.P., Nasre, R., Narayanaswamy, N.S.":::57355590000;35275730500;8935093600;":::Accelerating Computation of Steiner Trees on GPUs",2022
```

The code corresponding to this functionality uses two calls to re.search(), once for finding if an author is present (as any author) and another time as the first author.

```
match = re.search(author.upper(), authornames[ii].upper())
if match:
    match = re.search(r’”[^,]*’ + author.upper(), authornames[ii].upper())
    if not match: printRecord(ii)
```

**Functionality 5:** Find most prominent current and potential collaborators of an author.

This functionality is very different from the earlier ones. It involves identifying the most prominent current and potential collaborators of an author. For instance, we can identify with whom a given author has more publications (current collaborators). Further, to find potential collaborators, we can identify a common set of second-level collaborators from the direct collaborators. This is similar to how certain social networks suggest ‘People you may know’ – if your contacts have common contacts, it is likely that you would know them. Thus, if my collaborators collaborate with certain common people, those are likely to be my future collaborators.

For instance, for input ‘Nagarajan’, the output is:

```
{'Bhattacharya, S.': 129, 'Sharma, A.': 126, 'Wang, J.': 123, 'Kim, J.': 109, 'Wang, Z.': 90, 'Kumar, A.': 90, 'Ghosh, S.': 89, 'Zhang, Y.': 87, 'Lee, K.': 87, 'Jain, S.': 87}
```

Here we list the top 10 current and potential collaborators, along with their score (as a dictionary).

```
def getAllCollaborators(ii):
    collab = []
    names = authornames[ii].split(‘;’)
    newnn = ‘’
    ii = 0

    for nn in names:
    oldnn = newnn
        newnn = nn

        if newnn[0] == ‘“’: newnn = newnn[1:]
        if newnn[-1] == ‘”’: newnn = newnn[:-1]
        newnn = newnn.strip()

        if ii % 2 == 1:
            collab.append(oldnn + ‘, ‘ + newnn)
        ii = ii + 1

        return collab

def getCollab(author):
    directCollab = []

    for ii in range(len(authornames)):
        if author.upper() in authornames[ii].upper():
            directCollab = directCollab + getAllCollaborators(ii)
    return directCollab

def pcByCoauthors(author):
    directCollab = getCollab(author)
    collabCount = {}

    for dc in directCollab:
        indirectCollab = getCollab(dc)

        for indc in indirectCollab:
```

```
37.         if indc in collabCount: collabCount[indc] = collabCount[indc] + 1
38.         else: collabCount[indc] = 1
39.
40.     collabCount = dict(sorted(collabCount.items(), key = lambda kv: (kv[1], kv[0]),
        reverse=True))
41.     collabCount = dict(itertools.islice(collabCount.items(), 10))
42.
43.     print(collabCount)
```

The outer function *pcByCoauthors()* first collects direct collaborators using the function *getCollab()* in Line 34. For each of these direct collaborators, we find their collaborators in the loop at Line 36 (which are indirect collaborators of the original author). For each such indirect collaborator, we find the number of times it occurs via direct collaborators. This is naturally maintained in a dictionary (Lines 37 and 38). In the end, we soft this dictionary on these counts, from higher to lower values (Line 40). Out of these, we list the top 10 by slicing through the dictionary (Line 41), and print those (Line 43).

## UNIT SUMMARY

We learned to read and write to files, and to process those depending upon the application. We then digged deeper into various string related functions provided by the language. Finally, we explored the powerful world of regular expressions, allowing us to go beyond a simple find(). In each of these, we solved several problems.

## EXERCISES

### Multiple Choice Questions

1. Consider a text file data.txt whose contents are:

   Dean is Down with Dengue.

   What are the contents of data.txt after executing the following program?

```
fp = open("data.txt", "w+")
print("Dayalu Dean", file=fp)
fp.seek(7)
print("in Deen Dayal Nagar.", file=fp)
fp.close()
```

   (a) Dean is Down with Dengue.Dayalu in Deen Dayal Nagar.
   (b) Dayalu in Deen Dayal Nagar.
   (c) Dayalu Dean in Deen Dayal Nagar.
   (d) Dean is in Deen Dayal Nagar.

2. Consider a text file pqr.txt whose contents are:

   PQ RS

   What is the output of the following program?

```
fp = open("pqr.txt")
for text in fp.readline():
  print(text.lower())
fp.close()
```

(a) pq<br>rs

(b) p<br>q<br>r<br>s

(c) pq rs

(d) pqrs

3. What is the output of the following program?

```
text = "ToPsy TuRvy"
w1, w2 = text.split()
print(w1.swapcase(), w2.title().swapcase())
```

(a) tOpSY tUrVY

(b) tOpSY Turvy

(c) tOPSY tURVEY

(d) tOpSY tURVY

4. Which of the following regular expressions does NOT match 11/09/2023?

(a) \d\d/\d\d/\d{4}

(b) \w\w/\w\w/\d{4}

(c) \w\d\D\d\w\D\d\w\d\w

(d) \d\w\D\d\w\D\d\w\D\d

5. What is the output of the following program which works with HTML tags?

```
import re
html = "I am <b>NOT</b> going! You can do <b>whatever</b> you want"
match = re.findall('<.*>', html)
print(match[0])
```

(a) <b>NOT</b>

(b) </b>

(c) <b>NOT</b> going! You can do <b>whatever</b>

(d) <b>

| ANSWERS | | | | | | | | | |
|---|---|---|---|---|---|---|---|---|---|
| 1. | (b) | 2. | (b) | 3. | (d) | 4. | (d) | 5. | (c) |

## PRACTICAL

1. Extend our academic record maintenance program to work with multiple files corresponding to multiple students.
2. Extend our friends module to track age. Does the same program with minor modifications work, or do you need some more changes?
3. Modify our regular expression program to disallow email addresses of this type: *rupesh@iitm........a*. Thus, there should not be consecutive dots in the domain.
4. Create the regular expression for a URL.
5. Combine our file handling and regular expressions to implement a functionality similar to the *grep* utility, which finds lines having a pattern in a text file.

## Dynamic QR Code for Further Reading

# 5 Django Framework

## UNIT SPECIFICS

Through this unit we will discuss the following aspects:

- Installing and configuring the Django framework
- Creating a web application using the framework
- Passing parameters to the web application

## RATIONALE

Several ready-to-use frameworks have been developed using Python and are quite popular, such as Django, Web2Py, Ruby on Rails, etc. In this unit, we would like to explore a popular framework Django which allows us to build and run web applications. This would convey to you the power of using Python frameworks and how easy it is to develop your applications with them.

## PRE-REQUISITE

Units 1, 2, 3 and 4

## UNIT OUTCOMES

List of outcomes of this unit is as follows:

**U5-O1:** Install and configure Django framework

**U5-O2:** Create a project and an app in Django

**U5-O3:** Use the web application via a browser

| Unit-5 Outcomes | EXPECTED MAPPING WITH COURSE OUTCOMES (1- Weak Correlation; 2- Medium correlation; 3- Strong Correlation) | | | | | |
|---|---|---|---|---|---|---|
| | CO-1 | CO-2 | CO-3 | CO-4 | CO-5 | CO-6 |
| U5-O1 | 3 | 3 | 3 | – | 3 | 1 |
| U5-O2 | 1 | 1 | 2 | 2 | 1 | – |
| U5-O3 | 2 | 1 | 3 | 1 | 2 | 1 |

Building a web application has become quite easy with frameworks such as Django. Barring a few simple updates to files and executing a few commands, one can completely focus on creating the web content. In this unit, we will learn how to install and configure the Django framework, and then create our web applications.

## 5.1 INSTALLING AND RUNNING DJANGO

If Django is not already installed, it can be readily installed with the usual commands. For instance, on Linux, the following command can be used.

```
sudo apt install python3-django
```

On Windows, it is a two step process. In the first, we create a virtual environment, and then we can install Django via pip installer, as follows. All these commands can be executed either in cmd command prompt in Windows or in its PowerShell.

```
python -m venv myvenv
myvenv\Scripts\activate
python -m pip install Django
```

The first command creates a virtual environment in the directory myvenv. The second command activates it. The third command uses pip to install the Django framework.

To check if Django is already installed or whether it got installed correctly, try running the following command from your home directory (a directory you have write access to).

```
django-admin startproject mydjango
```

Here, mydjango is a project name of your choice. If the command runs successfully, it would not show any output, but will create the following directory structure.

```
$ ls -R mydjango/
mydjango/:
db.sqlite3  manage.py  mydjango
mydjango/mydjango:
asgi.py __init__.py __pycache__ settings.py urls.py wsgi.py
mydjango/mydjango/__pycache__:
__init__.cpython-38.pyc settings.cpython-38.pyc urls.cpython-38.pyc wsgi.cpython-38.pyc
```

For now, ignore the use of various files and subdirectories. We will get back to them as we create our first web application. But these files should indicate that Django is installed properly. We can now start the server.

```
$ cd mydjango
$ python3 manage.py runserver
Watching for file changes with StatReloader
Performing system checks...
System check identified no issues (0 silenced).
You have 18 unapplied migration(s). Your project may not work properly until you apply the
migrations for app(s): admin, auth, contenttypes, sessions.
Run 'python manage.py migrate' to apply them.
September 18, 2022 - 07:04:38
Django version 4.1.1, using settings 'mydjango.settings'
Starting development server at http://127.0.0.1:8000/
Quit the server with CONTROL-C.
_
```

This starts the server on the local machine at port 8000. The IP address to be used in the browser is highlighted above. We can think about the web-user as a client and *manage.py* as the server. To communicate, they both need to speak the same language, which is HTTP. Of course, the user does not need to understand what HTTP commands are – that gets done by our browser.

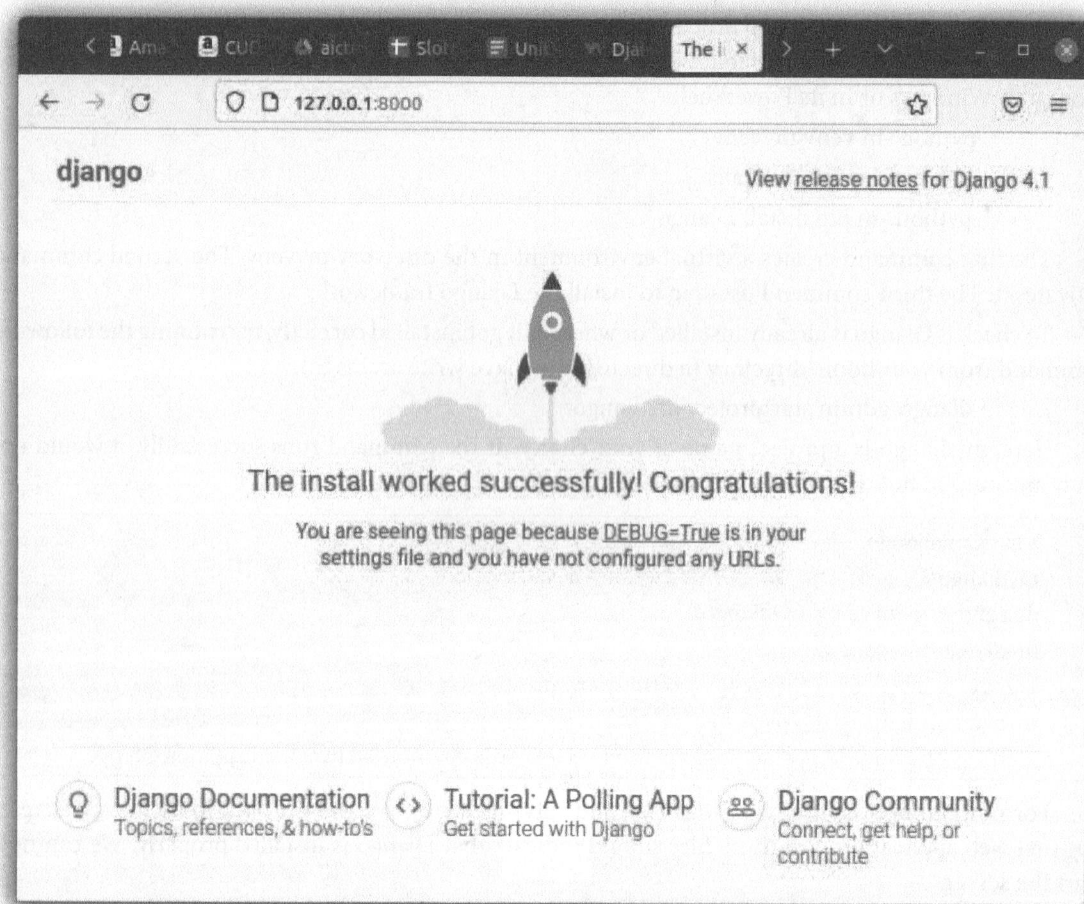


If the installation is unsuccessful or the server is not running, the browser will issue the usual message: *Unable to connect.* Note that since the browser and the web server are running on the same machine (your laptop or desktop), an internet connection is not required to check this. 127.0.0.1 is a special IP address which refers to the local machine. If all is well, the browser would show a rocket and the server running on the command-line will issue a message similar to the following:

```
[18/Sep/2022 07:06:24] "GET / HTTP/1.1" 200 10681
```

## 5.2 CREATING AND RUNNING A WEB APPLICATION

We are now ready to create our first web application. Navigate to the mydjango directory (where manage.py exists) and issue the following command.

```
$ python3 manage.py startapp appone
```

This is our first web application, named appone. You will see the corresponding directory created in the current directory, with the following structure.

```
$ ls -R appone/
appone/:
admin.py apps.py __init__.py migrations models.py tests.py views.py
appone/migrations:
__init__.py
```

Let's see if this is sufficient to run our webapp appone. We restart the server.

```
$ python3 manage.py runserver
```

and in our web-browser, we enter the same url: http://127.0.0.1:8000/

This works as before (with the rocket sign). This means we have not broken anything (so far). Now we check appone by entering the url in the browser as: http://127.0.0.1:8000/appone

This shows the browser screen as below.

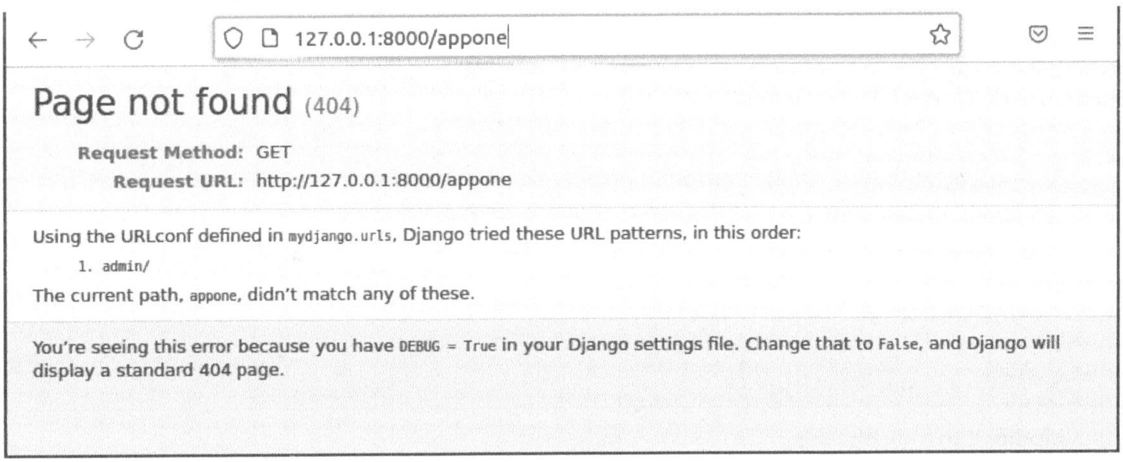


This indicates that the web-server manage.py is unable to find appone. This is because, although the directory appone exists, it needs to be registered explicitly.

**App Registration Step 1:** Open *mydjango/mydjango/urls.py* file. It should originally look as below.

```
...
from django.contrib import admin
from django.urls import path
urlpatterns = [
    path('admin/', admin.site.urls),
]
```

Modify it to the following.

```
...
from django.contrib import admin
from django.urls import path, include

urlpatterns = [
    path(‘admin/’, admin.site.urls),
    path(‘appone/’, include(‘appone.urls’)),
]
```

At this stage, the server may issue certain errors (e.g., ModuleNotFoundError: No module named ‘appone.urls’). Ignore the errors for now. If we try to check again in the browser, we may encounter *Unable to connect* message. This means the registration of our web-app is not yet complete.

**App Registration Step 2:** This time, we need to create the appone directory’s *urls.py* file (note that the file is not already present). This file permits accessing the contents of *appone’s views.py*.

```
from django.urls import path
from . import views

urlpatterns = [
    path(“, views.index, name=’index’),
]
```

At this stage, the server may issue other errors (e.g., AttributeError: module ‘appone.views’ has no attribute ‘index’). This indicates that the registration needs additional steps.

**App Registration Step 3:** Open the file *appone/views.py*. It exists and should look like this.

```
from django.shortcuts import render

# Create your views here.
```

Modify it to look like this.

```
from django.shortcuts import render
from django.http import HttpResponse

def index(request):
    return HttpResponse(“<h1>Hello World!</h1>”)
```

Restart the server (by going to *mydjango* directory):

```
$ python3 manage.py runserver
```

At this stage, the server should not issue any errors. Open the url in the browser and it should print *Hello World!*

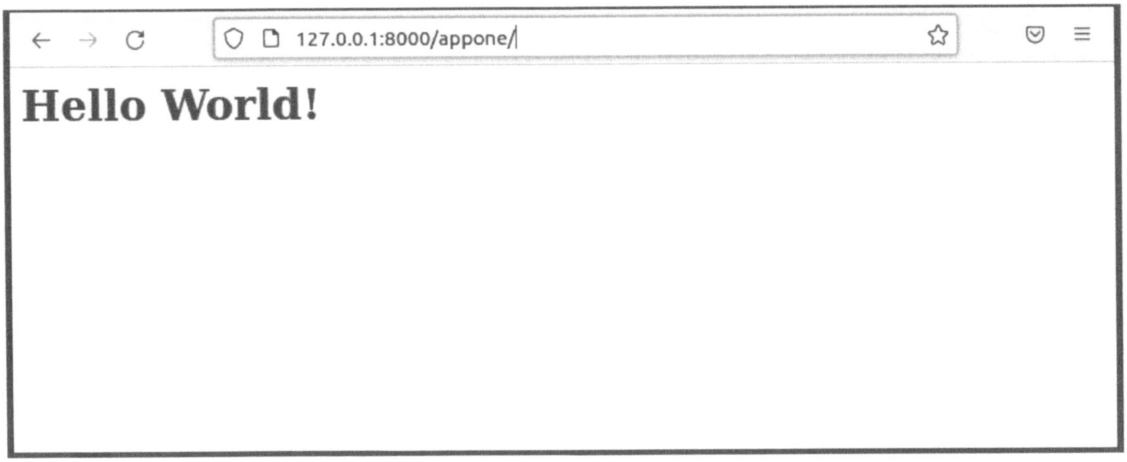


Once this basic setup is running, we can add arbitrary HTML text and can process it from *views.py*.

**Example:** Display an HTML file.

Let's create a simple HTML file in appone directory, named *basic.html*. Its contents are as follows. We will assume that you know basic HTML.

**basic.html**

```
<h2>This is basic HTML</h2>
It contains <a href='http://www.cse.iitm.ac.in/~rupesh/books/python/'>a link to Python
Programming's webpage</a>, and an image of Python Logo.<p>
<img src='https://www.python.org/static/img/psf-logo.png'><p>
Do you know that we can also create tables in it?<p>
<table border=1>
    <tr><td>one one</td><td>one two</td></tr>
    <tr><td>two one</td><td>two two</td></tr>
</table>
<p>
That's all for now.
```

You can open this file in a browser to see how it looks. But we would like our webapp to show this content. Keeping everything else the same, let's modify *appone/views.py* file as follows.

```
from django.shortcuts import render
from django.http import HttpResponse

def index(request):
    fp = open('/home/rupesh/mydjango/appone/basic.html')
    htmlstr = fp.read()
    fp.close()

    return HttpResponse(htmlstr)
```

We use our file handling functions to read *basic.html* as a string, and return it as the HTTP response (when the browser issues an HTTP request to our server).

**Important Note:** The file path provided in Line 5 needs to be an absolute path, unless Django settings allow a relative path.

When viewed in a browser, the contents of basic.html are visible.

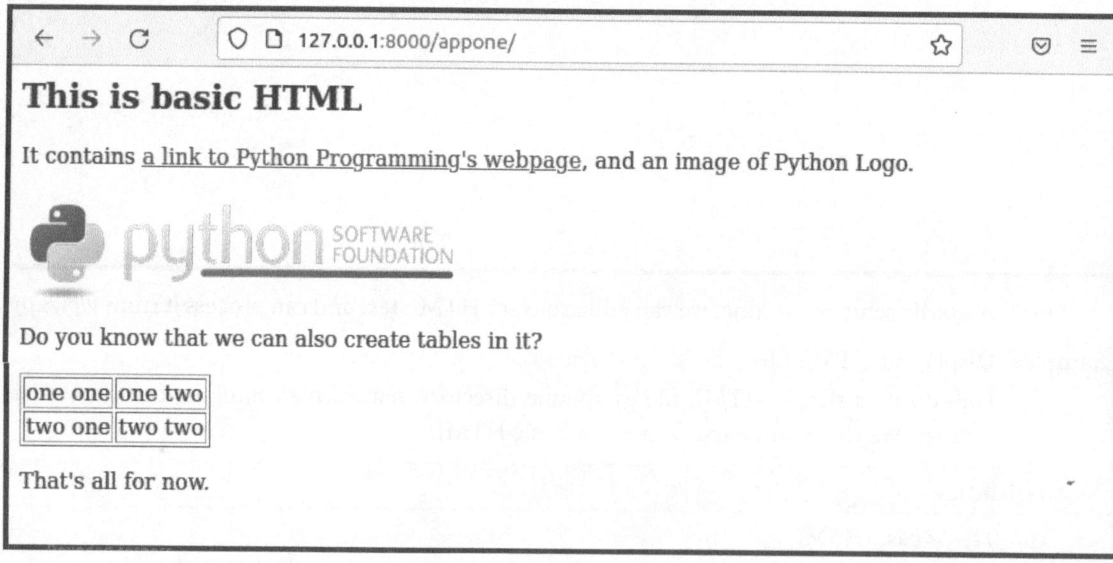


Note that from the *index()* function of views.py, we can use arbitrary Python code to perform application-specific processing. For instance, changing Line 9 to

```
return HttpResponse(htmlstr.lower())
```

changes all the text to lowercase.

**Example:** Display academic record using a web-app.

Recall our academic record programs. We stored the course number, its credits, and earned credits in a file, and read this information to populate in our lists. We then also computed CGPA and printed this information on the screen. In this unit, we will modify the functionality to print this as an HTML table. Let's create a new application for this.

**Step 0:** Create the app from *mydjango* directory.

```
$ python3 manage.py startapp acads
```

**Step 1:** Adding entry to *mydjango/mydjango/urls.py*

```
from django.contrib import admin
from django.urls import path, include

urlpatterns = [
    path('admin/', admin.site.urls),
    path('appone/', include('appone.urls')),
    path('acads/', include('acads.urls')),
]
```

**Step 2:** Creating *acads/urls.py* (you can copy it from *appone/urls.py*)

```
from django.urls import path
from . import views

urlpatterns = [
    path('', views.index, name='index'),
]
```

**Step 3:** Writing code in *acads/views.py*

```
from django.shortcuts import render
from django.http import HttpResponse
from .academics import *

def processAcads(filename):
    htmlstr = '<table border=1>\n'
    acadfile = open(filename)

    for line in acadfile:
        if line == '\n':# new semester
            htmlstr = htmlstr + gethtml()
            htmlstr = htmlstr + "<tr><td colspan=3>This Sem CGPA:" + \
                        str(cgpa()) + "</td></tr>\n"
        else:
            cc, cr, ea = line.split()
            add(cc, int(cr), int(ea))

    acadfile.close()
    htmlstr = htmlstr + '</table><br>\n'
    return htmlstr

def index(request):
    htmlstr = processAcads("/home/rupesh/mydjango/acads/academics.txt")
    return HttpResponse(htmlstr)
```

Note that we have imported the same module academics, but we have added a function *gethtml()* to get the HTML version of an academic record.

**Step 4:** Start the server from *mydjango* directory.

```
$ python3 manage.py runserver
```

**Step 5:** Access the academic record from the browser. Enter the URL as:

```
http://127.0.0.1:8000/acads/
```

The browser should display the academic record as follows:

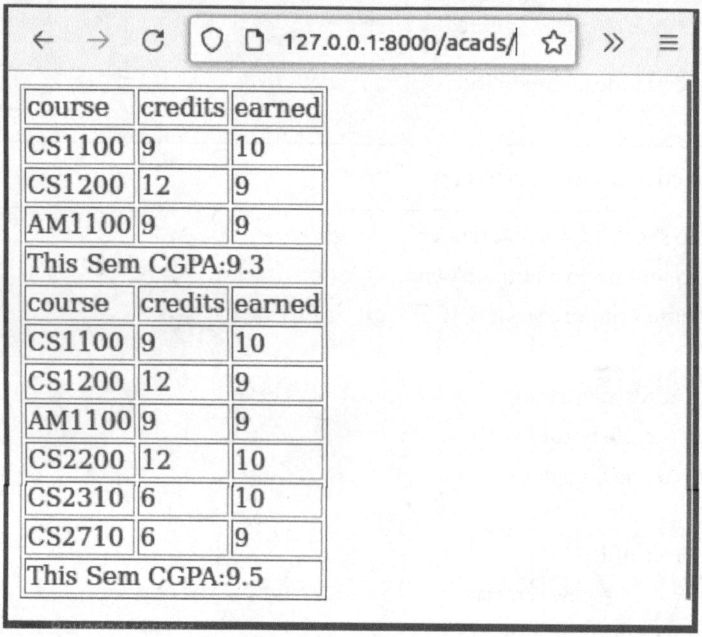


| course | credits | earned |
|---|---|---|
| CS1100 | 9 | 10 |
| CS1200 | 12 | 9 |
| AM1100 | 9 | 9 |
| This Sem CGPA:9.3 | | |
| course | credits | earned |
| CS1100 | 9 | 10 |
| CS1200 | 12 | 9 |
| AM1100 | 9 | 9 |
| CS2200 | 12 | 10 |
| CS2310 | 6 | 10 |
| CS2710 | 6 | 9 |
| This Sem CGPA:9.5 | | |

## 5.3 PARAMETER PASSING WITH GET

Users can pass parameters to our web-app. For instance, we can write an app for exponentiation (it is an overkill, but this is an example). One can then invoke the program as:

```
http://127.0.0.1:8000/expo/?x=2&y=8
```

The parameters are named, are assigned values using = operator, and are separated by &. In *expo/views.py*, we can then extract the values of *x* and *y*, compute *x**y* and print the value in the HTTP response. Django provides a dictionary *GET* within its HTTP request to access these variables.

```
def index(request):
    x = int(request.GET['x'])
    y = int(request.GET['y'])
    return HttpResponse(str(x**y))
```

The output shown on the browser will be

```
256
```

You can experiment with other values. Let's make use of such parameter passing functionality to create our Django webpage.

**Example:** Create a personal webpage.

Our webpage should have the following display elements.

- A common header containing a photo and basic affiliation information.
- A common menu to navigate through Home, Academics, Projects, and Contacts.
- When we click on a particular menu item, appropriate information should be displayed below the menu.

Sample screenshots of our personal webpage are shown below. The first screen shows the landing Home page.

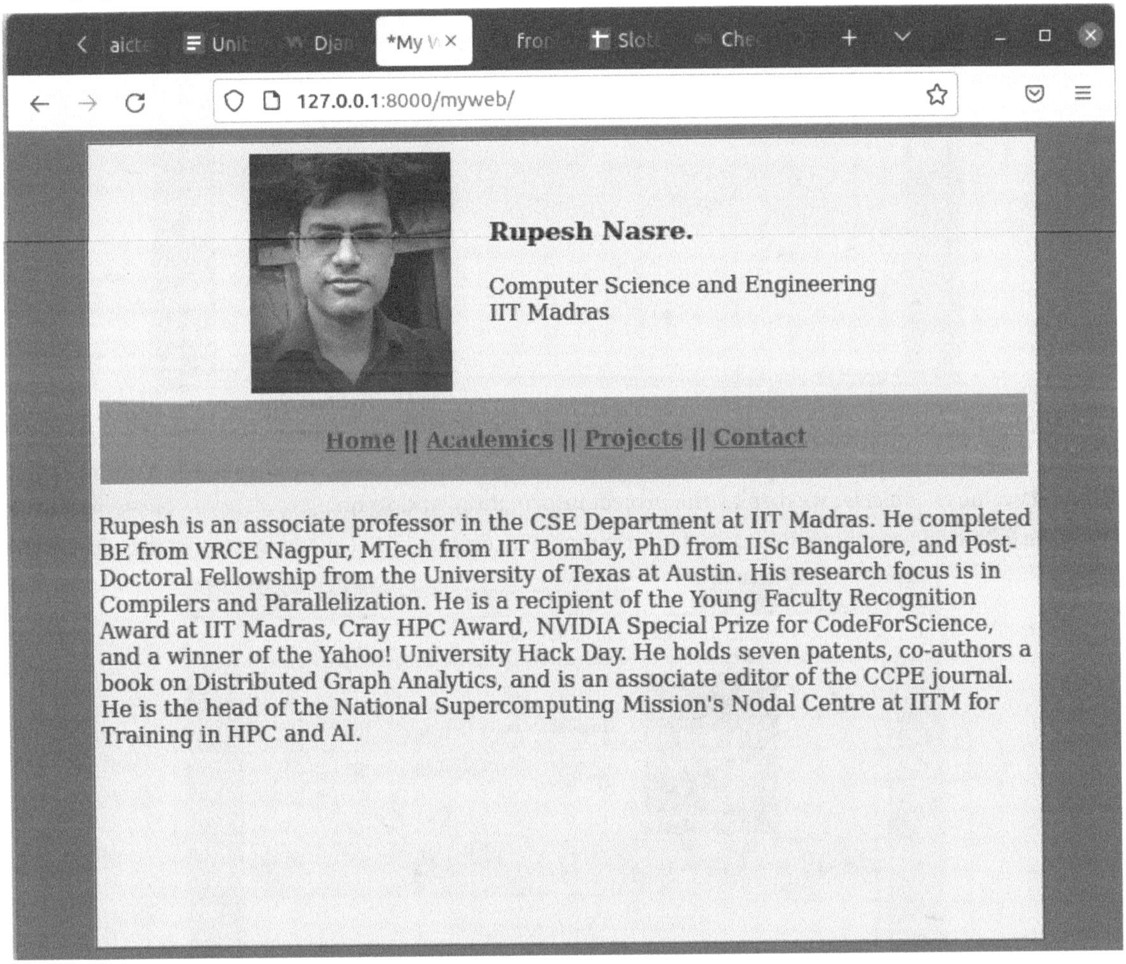


Note the URL in the address bar. The next page is about Projects.

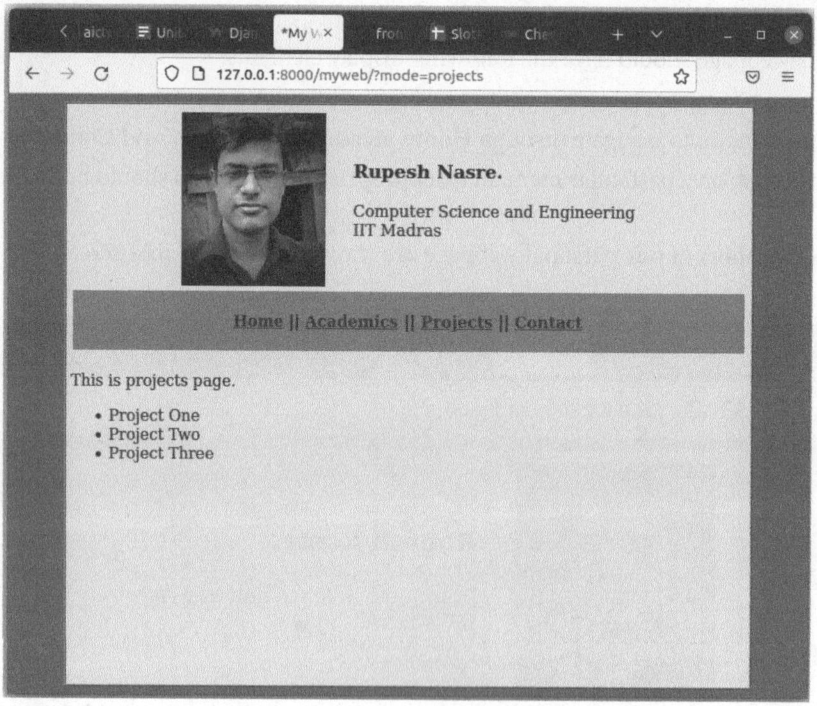


Note how the address-bar shows the parameters passed. We use a parameter named *mode* whose value decides which page to show. When *mode* was undefined or *'home'*, we displayed the home page. When its value is *'projects'*, we display the project information, and so on.

The following page shows the contact information. Once again, notice *mode=contact* in the address bar.

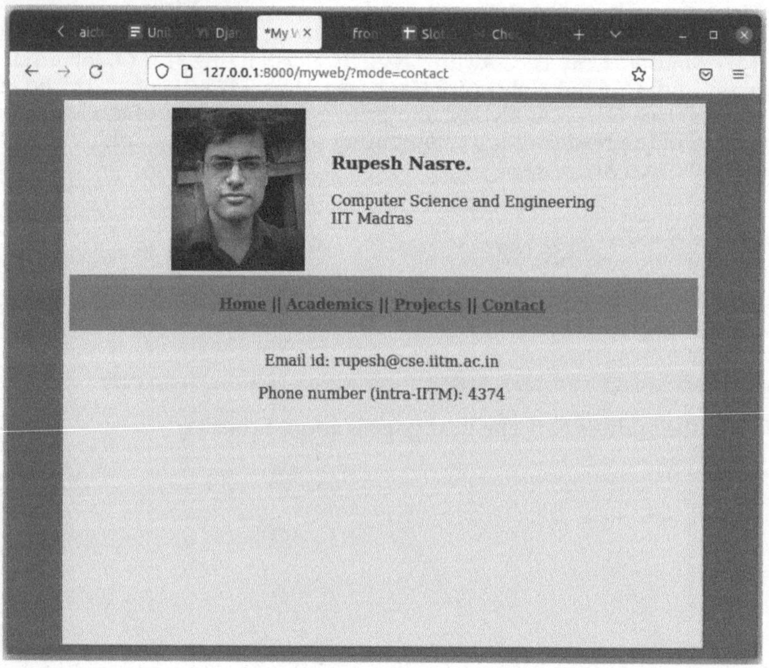

Creating such a menu system is straightforward in HTML. We show the header and the footer below, which are common across all the displayed pages.

**header.html**

```
<head>
        <title>*My Webpage with DJango*</title>
</head>
<body bgcolor='#44aa44'>
<table align=center width=700 border=1 cellpadding=5 cellspacing=0 bgcolor='#ddffee'
height=100%><tr><td valign=top>
<table align=center><tr><td>
<img src='http://www.cse.iitm.ac.in/~rupesh/media/rupesh.jpg' width=150><br>
        </td><td width=20>
                 
        </td><td>
                <h3>Rupesh Nasre.</h3>
                Computer Science and Engineering<br>
                IIT Madras<br>
        </td></tr></table>
<table align=center width=700><tr><td bgcolor='#66cc66' align=center>
                <br><b> <a href='?mode=home'>Home</a> ||
                <a href='?mode=acads'>Academics</a> ||
                <a href='?mode=projects'>Projects</a> ||
                <a href='?mode=contact'>Contact</a> </b><br> 
</td></tr></table><br>
```

Notice how we have specified mode values while creating links for Home, Academics, Projects, and Contact.

**footer.html**

```
</td></tr></table>
</body>
```

Files *home.html*, *acads.html*, *projects.html*, and *contact.html* are simpler. We show one of them. These files do not contain any Python code.

**home.html**

Rupesh is an associate professor in the CSE Department at IIT Madras. He completed BE from VRCE Nagpur, MTech from IIT Bombay, PhD from IISc Bangalore, and Post-Doctoral Fellowship from the University of Texas at Austin. His research focus is in Compilers and Parallelization. He is a recipient of the Young Faculty Recognition Award at IIT Madras, Cray HPC Award, NVIDIA Special Prize for CodeForScience, and a winner of the Yahoo! University Hack Day. He holds seven patents, co-authors a book on Distributed Graph Analytics, and is an associate editor of the CCPE journal. He is the head of the National Supercomputing Mission's Nodal Centre at IITM for Training in HPC and AI.

Who glues these files together? It is the *views.py* file from *myweb* directory, which gets invoked when we load a particular page from the browser, which also takes care of reading the *mode* parameter.

**myweb/views.py**

```
1.  from django.shortcuts import render
2.  from django.http import HttpResponse
3.
4.  def index(request):
5.      if ‘mode’ in request.GET:
6.          mode = request.GET[‘mode’]
7.      else:
8.          mode = ‘home’
9.
10.     folder = ‘/home/rupesh/mydjango/myweb/’
11.     header = ‘header.html’
12.     footer = ‘footer.html’
13.     filename = folder + mode + ‘.html’
14.
15.     htmlstr = ‘’
16.     fp = open(folder + header)          # display header
17.     htmlstr = htmlstr + fp.read()
18.     fp.close()
19.
20.     fp = open(filename)                 # display mode file
21.     htmlstr = htmlstr + fp.read()
22.     fp.close()
23.
24.     fp = open(folder + footer)          # display footer
25.     htmlstr = htmlstr + fp.read()
26.     fp.close()
27.
28.     return HttpResponse(htmlstr)
```

Lines 5–8 read the *mode* parameter, if defined. While displaying, the HTML is formed from three different files: header, mode file, and footer. This is shown in further processing. A concatenation of all three HTML files is finally sent as the HTTP response (Line 28).

## UNIT SUMMARY

We learned to installed and configure Django. We then created our web-applications to output HTML from our Python programs. Django is a framework which allows us to create these applications easily. Finally, we learned how to pass parameters to our Python web-application, which allows customized processing.

# EXERCISES

## Multiple Choice Questions

1. After successful installation of Django, I start the server, but when I try to connect to the server from my browser using URL http://127.0.0.1/, I am unable to connect. What is the reason?
   (a) Server is started from a wrong location. (b) IP address is wrong.
   (c) Port is wrong. (d) Internet is unavailable.
2. Consider the following Django function in *views.py*, which reads from a file in the same directory.

```
def index(request):
    fp = open("file.html")
    htmlstr = fp.read()
    fp.close()
    return HttpResponse(htmlstr.lower())
```

   What will be the output of this function (when invoked appropriately from the browser)?
   (a) No output
   (b) Error that the file is not found
   (c) Contents of file.html are displayed in lower-case.
   (d) Error that the contents of file.html are modified
3. Which of the following steps is not required to create and start a new application named newapp?
   (a) Executing *python3 manage.py startapp newapp*
   (b) Updating *mydjango/mydjango/urls.py*
   (d) Updating *newapp/views.py*
   (d) Updating *newapp/migrate.py*
4. What URL will produce output 20 for the following Django program in an application named *prod*?

```
def index(request):
    val = int(request.GET['one']) * int(request.GET['two'])
    return HttpResponse(str(val))
```

   (a) http://127.0.0.1:8000/prod/?x=2&y=10
   (b) http://127.0.0.1:8000/prod/?one=one&two=twenty
   (c) http://127.0.0.1:8000/prod/?one=5&two=2
   (d) http://127.0.0.1:8000/prod/?two=5&one=4
5. What is the output of the following program when invoked with URL http://127.0.0.1:8000/myweb/?tag=bold&beautiful

```
def index(request):
    return HttpResponse(request.GET['tag'].upper())
```

(a) BOLD&BEAUTIFUL (b) BOLD

(c) BEAUTIFUL (d) Browser Error

| ANSWERS | | | | | | | | | |
|---|---|---|---|---|---|---|---|---|---|
| 1. | (c) | 2. | (b) | 3. | (d) | 4. | (d) | 5. | (b) |

## PRACTICAL

1. Modify our personal webpage such that when a menu item's page is displayed, the corresponding menu item is displayed as a plain-text, and not as a hyperlink. For instance, when we click on Projects, the menu should be displayed as:

   **Home || Academics || Projects || Contact**

2. Extend our academics program to multiple students, with a particular student's roll number passed as a GET parameter.
3. Create a webpage to display items of a shop. Allow filters by category or price.
4. Extend our conference related Python application (from Unit 4) to display the information as a web-app.
5. Create a web-application for various numerical problems (sum of numbers, product of a series, powers of two, solving an equation, etc.). Users can choose a method using a parameter.

## Dynamic QR Code for Further Reading

## REFERENCES FOR FURTHER LEARNING

The best way to learn Python is by trying out programs yourself.

Following are certain references which I have found useful. There must be other numerous very good references as well.


1. Guido van Rossum and the Python development team, Python Tutorial, Python Software Foundation, 2018
2. Brian Heinold, A Practical Introduction to Python Programming, Creative Commons, 2012
3. w3schools, Python Tutorial, online https://www.w3schools.com/python/default.asp
4. Codes from Geeks For Geeks https://www.geeksforgeeks.org/python-programming-examples/
5. Course webpage (codes / errata for this book, and more examples) http://www.cse.iitm.ac.in/~rupesh/books/python/_

## CO AND PO ATTAINMENT TABLE

Course outcomes (COs) for this course can be mapped with the programme outcomes (POs) after the completion of the course and a correlation can be made for the attainment of POs to analyze the gap. After proper analysis of the gap in the attainment of POs necessary measures can be taken to overcome the gaps.

**Table for CO and PO attainment**

| Course Outcomes | Attainment of Programme Outcomes *(1- Weak Correlation; 2- Medium correlation; 3- Strong Correlation)* | | | | | | |
|---|---|---|---|---|---|---|---|
| | PO-1 | PO-2 | PO-3 | PO-4 | PO-5 | PO-6 | PO-7 |
| CO-1 | 3 | 3 | 3 | 2 | 1 | 1 | 2 |
| CO-2 | 3 | 3 | 3 | 2 | 1 | 1 | 2 |
| CO-3 | 3 | 3 | 3 | 2 | 1 | 1 | 2 |
| CO-4 | 3 | 3 | 3 | 2 | 1 | 1 | 2 |
| CO-5 | 3 | 3 | 3 | 2 | 1 | 1 | 2 |

The data filled in the above table can be used for gap analysis.

# INDEX